UNDERSTANDING YOUNG
CHILDREN'S BEHAVIOUR

UNDERSTANDING YOUNG CHILDREN'S BEHAVIOUR

A guide for early childhood professionals

Jillian Rodd

ALLEN & UNWIN

Every effort has been made to acknowledge the source of material that is not original in this book. However, many of the terms and the concepts are so commonly used that the original source is uncertain. The author and publisher would be pleased to hear from copyright holders to rectify any omissions or errors.

Copyright © Jillian Rodd 1996

First published in 1996 by
Allen & Unwin Pty Ltd
9 Atchison Street, St Leonards, NSW 2065 Australia
Phone: (61 2) 9901 4088
Fax: (61 2) 9906 2218
E-mail: 100252.103@compuserve.com

National Library of Australia
Cataloguing-in-Publication entry:

Rodd, Jillian, 1949– .
  Understanding young children's behaviour: strategies for early childhood professionals.

  Bibliography.
  Includes indexes.
  ISBN 1 86448 163 3.

  1. Early childhood education. 2. Child development. I. Title.

372.21

Set in Optima and 10.5/12 pt Garamond by DOCUPRO, Sydney
Printed by KHL Printing Co Pte Limited, Singapore

10 9 8 7 6 5 4 3 2 1

For my son
Julian Rodd Maskell:
the phoenix has risen.

Contents

Acknowledgements

My interest in this topic came out of my experiences with my own children when they were young. As a young and inexperienced mother of two, I wanted to be calm and in control, kind and loving, know how to respond to and be able to manage their behaviour, have a loving relationship with them and be positive and optimistic with and about my children and my parenting. By the time my son was nine, it felt as if I was the opposite of all that I had wanted to be! Even though I was a trained psychologist, it took me all of those years to understand that I could learn how to be more effective in managing young children's behaviour. I am a slow learner in some areas of my life! Because of my experience, I want to acknowledge the role that my children, Julian and Claudia Maskell, played in my ongoing interest in this area and thank them for giving me the impetus to learn about behaviour management of young children.

During the time my children were growing up, I was working as an academic in the early childhood field in Melbourne. From visits to centres and discussion with practising members in the field, including students, I became aware of the impact of ineffective behaviour management practices upon the day to day running of early childhood centres and on the self esteem and job satisfaction of early childhood professionals. In fact, many early childhood professionals were expressing the same concerns about their behaviour management abilities as I had as a young mother!

I wish to acknowledge that my understanding about behaviour management is a reflection of the accumulated experience that many early childhood professionals have shared with me. A hallmark of the members of the Australian early childhood field is their willingness to reflect upon their practices and share their expertise.

Finally, I wish to thank my husband, Gerald Gray, for his encouragement of and support for my writing and for tolerating my working so intensively on this book in the first year of our marriage.

Introduction

The moment that an early childhood professional takes responsibility for and charge of an individual child or group of children, be they student or employee, qualified or unqualified, experienced or inexperienced with young children, the challenge of behaviour management begins. Young children do not give early childhood professionals the liberty or freedom to ignore this aspect of their role or to defer responding to behavioural incidents until they feel more comfortable, confident, knowledgeable and skilled. Professional requirements and obligations to protect children from danger, including harming themselves, and to enhance children's welfare and well being, including their development and learning, mean that early childhood professionals need to be prepared to respond promptly to young children's behaviour in ways that maintain positive relationships, self esteem and create opportunities for learning.

Today's children are growing up in a rapidly changing society which makes demands on them for early cooperative, mature and independent behaviour that have not been made to the same extent on previous generations of children. The current generation of young children will spend many hours of the first five years of their lives in group care and education settings. Because of the sheer quantity of time that these children spend outside the home and away from parents, they will be socialised largely by non familial adults, such as family day care providers, child care workers and preschool teachers. Community concern about the number of hours young children are spending under the control of early childhood professionals and the quality of childhood that they experience when in group care has led to interest in how the adults who are responsible for them manage their behaviour and help them learn how to become fully functioning, contributing and responsible members of their culture and society.

The recent concern about and interest in young children and their behaviour stems from the higher levels of education throughout the general community which have provided people with some knowledge about the importance of adult–child interaction and child development. Families are having fewer children and children are becoming more precious. Yet, at the same time, the upsurge in reports of physical, emotional and sexual abuse of young children is an indication of the difficulties some adults have in relating and responding to young children and their behaviour. Those adults who are concerned with young children's development, learning and welfare, such as parents and early childhood professionals, want to provide young children with the best possible upbringing in order that they possess the skills to function effectively in society.

Living in today's society can be very stressful for both young children, their parents and the early childhood professionals who are concerned with children and families. Some of this stress comes from the pace and demands of modern life, but in relation to young children's behaviour, one particular source of stress is the lack of tradition in child rearing and behaviour management practices. In previous generations, child rearing techniques which had been proven over time were passed on to the next generation of parents and child minders as established traditions for meeting the typical situations and incidents encountered during daily life. The task of responding to young children's behaviour was not difficult because 'recipe' techniques were readily at hand. However, the tendency to revert to more traditional authoritarian and punitive forms of behaviour management can pose a problem for those who work with young children. Despite the fact that the use of physical punishment by early childhood professionals is prohibited by law in Australia as well as in many other countries, some early childhood professionals still engage in practices which would be considered against the law and even as child abuse. Hitting, shaking, pinching, squeezing, standing a child in the corner, locking a child in a cupboard, tying a child to a high chair or cot, shouting at, yelling at, humiliating the child or any other degrading practices may be construed as abusive. It is therefore essential that early childhood professionals learn more appropriate ways of managing young children's behaviour and incorporate such practices as part of a policy statement on behaviour management within the curriculum.

Nevertheless, despite increased knowledge about children's development and the demands of modern living, responding appropriately to young children's need for guidance and discipline has become difficult and challenging for many adults, including parents and early childhood professionals. We live in a society which has a pluralistic value system. That is, there is not one clear set of values to guide behaviour but many different and equally legitimate value systems to adopt and follow. Because the traditional authoritarian values and methods of raising children often are no longer considered to be acceptable in terms of young children's physical and psychological well being, adults who live and work with young children simply do not know what to do (Balson, 1994). They know that the traditional ways are unsuitable for this generation of children, yet they have not found other approaches which reflect more democratic and humanistic values on which to base their guidance, discipline and behaviour management techniques.

Early childhood professionals have a special responsibility to ensure that they interact with young children and respond to their behaviour in ways that reflect community values, expectations, standards, norms and rules. Because they work within a defined professional field, known as the early years or early childhood, these professionals are also required to act in ways consistent with currently accepted professional values. These demands, as well as the nature of young children and their behaviour, make effective behaviour management a challenging aspect of the job.

It is easy for early childhood professionals, the majority of whom are qualified and experienced in working with young children, to feel frustrated and defeated by the seemingly inconsistent and unpredictable outcomes of their attempts to manage children's behaviour. They need to remember that each child is a unique individual who brings with her to the early childhood centre an amalgam of inherited characteristics, family and cultural values and orientations, societal influences and their own life experiences. Young children's behaviour is also influenced by the immediate, concrete situational context and cues within that context (Rodd, 1988). Young children differ in their sensitivity and responsivity to contextual cues related to displays of acceptable and unacceptable behaviour. Early childhood professionals need to be aware that features of the environment can act to help or hinder the display of appropriate behaviour. Finally, the type of problem behaviour that young children display can influence the success of the early childhood professional's behaviour management efforts. Some behaviours, such as biting and aggression appear to be more resistant to discipline techniques. Occasionally, the early childhood professional's best intentions and practices simply do not work! Understanding that some children, situations and problems are really very difficult to manage effectively can help early childhood professionals cope better when their strategies do not work out as planned or when results seem to be slow in coming.

Because effective behaviour management with young children is such a challenge for early childhood professionals, it is important that they are able to realistically assess their competence and limitations in the area and acknowledge when a situation is beyond their present abilities. Rather than being regarded as a sign of weakness and failure on their part, recognition of one's limitations, followed by further training and practice, is a sign of professionalism. It is important to become a 'learning person' in relation to behaviour management because children, families, cultures and societies are changing constantly. Adults can always learn something new for managing young children's behaviour more effectively, be it from training, reading, discussion with others or self evaluation and reflective practice. Even referral of a child to a different type of early childhood centre—for example, from a large group long day care centre to a family day care home—is a professional way of showing care and respect for meeting the individual and special needs of the child.

The contents of this book reflect selected issues and skills associated with the effective management of behaviour in children from birth to approximately five years of age. It was written to give current and intending practitioners a better understanding of the nature of behaviour management in early childhood settings and discusses specific issues related to the implementation of a positive approach to discipline and behaviour management.

Chapter 1 explores the nature of the challenge that behaviour management poses to early childhood professionals, identifies broad categories of inappropriate behaviour that early childhood professionals are likely to encounter in their work, considers some of the commonly used terms related to behaviour management, differentiates power-assertive, love withdrawal and inductive reasoning approaches to behaviour management, defines discipline and behaviour management for early childhood settings and summarises some of the basic facts about working with young children that underpin the development of a personal yet professional approach to behaviour management.

Chapter 2 reviews some of the key characteristics of normal child development to familiarise early childhood professionals with the developmental capabilities and limitations associated with particular stages of development from birth to five years. The relationship of physical and language development to behaviour management is discussed with attention given to the areas of emotional, social and intellectual development.

Chapter 3 highlights the development of self concept and self esteem as critical aspects of development which are related to approaches to behaviour management. The dimensions which make up self esteem, that is, competence, control, worth, connection and contribution, are discussed and guidelines for enhancing the development of self concept and self esteem in approaches to behaviour management are provided.

Chapter 4 examines young children's understanding of right and wrong as aspects of developing self control and self discipline. The development of moral understanding and behaviour is discussed from a range of theoretical perspectives with the roles of empathy, perspective taking and distributive justice in young children's emerging moral reasoning outlined. A range of practical strategies for stimulating young children's moral understanding, reasoning and behaviour are offered.

Chapter 5 focuses upon the need for early childhood professionals to themselves understand what they want from young children in terms of defining expectations and goals. Behaviour management is examined as a fundamental part of the overall curriculum or program along with the need for the establishment of short term, long term and educational goals. The need for early childhood professionals to look for causes of inappropriate behaviour rather than reacting to symptoms is discussed as well as adult, child and mutual ownership of problems.

Chapter 6 pinpoints problem prevention as a key element in a positive approach to discipline and behaviour management. Factors in both the physical and emotional environments which contribute to a preventive approach to behaviour management are discussed as well as the importance of a developmentally appropriate, meaningful and enjoyable curriculum or program.

Chapter 7 outlines the detrimental effects which punishment as an approach to behaviour management can have upon young children and their development. The potential harmful side effects that punishment has upon young children's learning and self esteem are explained in detail so that early childhood professionals clearly understand the rationale behind the recommendation for the adoption of alternative approaches to discipline and behaviour management.

Chapter 8 highlights communication skills as essential in the implementation of approaches to behaviour management. The characteristics of a recommended positive style of communication are summarised. A number of principles which are considered to help early childhood professionals to communicate more effectively with young children are explained and a summary of helpful versus harmful communication techniques related to behaviour management is provided.

Chapter 9 brings together and describes a range of behaviour management strategies which are considered to contribute to a positive approach to discipline and guidance. A review of broad aims for behaviour management is provided as well as factors which need to be considered when choosing a behaviour management technique. Specific strategies for dealing with the behaviour of children under two years of age and children between two and five years are identified. Guidelines for and examples of the appropriate implementation of a selected range of positive discipline techniques are offered.

Chapter 10 discusses the importance of each early childhood professional creating a personal and professional system of behaviour management. The characteristics of behaviour management strategies and outcomes which are regarded as both desirable and professional are outlined, as are guidelines for creating a personal approach to behaviour management. The positive discipline strategies are summarised under specific goal and outcome categories.

These aim to prevent early problems from occurring, prevent later problems from developing, foster self control, encourage desired behaviour and discourage unacceptable behaviours. Finally, a short list of reminders about what to avoid doing and what to try to do when managing the behaviour of young children is offered.

This book is based upon over twenty years of personal and professional experience of living and working with young children as well as helping to prepare students, parents and early childhood professionals to understand and become more effective in behaviour management. It is written from an appreciation of the practical difficulties associated with managing young children's behaviour in early childhood centres and an understanding of the frequently occurring and common day to day incidents which early childhood professionals encounter in their work with young children. The book is intended to support, not to be critical of early childhood professionals in one of the most challenging and potentially satisfying aspects of their work, that is, behaviour management. Early childhood professionals who have access to a broad range of behaviour management strategies are likely to feel better resourced and more confident when responding to individual children and specific incidents.

The information, concepts and skills presented in this book are eclectic, that is, they are derived from and grounded in a range of theoretical perspectives including behavioural, humanistic and cognitive-developmental theory as well as Adlerian psychology. Although the strategies covered in this book might sometimes appear to be a blend of philosophically incompatible approaches, they reflect the reality of early childhood professionals' circumstances, where a broad range of strategies are required to meet the individual needs of children and specific situations. It is hoped that the reader will select those strategies that are most consistent with her philosophy, personality and situation. The concepts and skills have been presented in an applied and practical form in order to make the content accessible, meaningful and interesting for students, novices and seasoned early childhood professionals alike.

Because members of the early childhood field are moving away from differentiating between education and care and the terms 'teacher' and 'caregiver' do not represent the functions of those staff concerned with the care and early education of young children, the term 'early childhood professional' has been used to cover all members of the early childhood profession, including family day care providers, qualified and untrained child care workers, coordinators and directors and preschool or kindergarten teachers. In the same way, the term 'early childhood centre' has been used to include family day care homes, occasional, long day and work based child care centres, preschools, kindergartens and early learning centres. While not wishing to display gender bias, female terminology is used generally throughout this book when referring to 'the child' in general as well as to the early childhood professional. This reflects the fact that the overwhelming majority of early childhood professionals in Australia and throughout the world are women. It in no way is meant to reflect upon the important and valuable contribution made by the caring men who work in early childhood centres. In an effort to eliminate gender bias as well as the clumsy use of 'his/her' or 'their' when referring to 'the child', 'the infant' or 'the toddler', I have chosen to use the personal pronoun 'she' as a generic term.

1

GUIDING CHILDREN'S BEHAVIOUR

The challenge for adults

One of the greatest challenges for anyone who lives and works with young children is to respond to and manage their behaviour in ways that are satisfying and productive for all concerned. Working with young children is physically, intellectually and emotionally demanding especially for early childhood professionals who work with a range of children, from those who are normal to those with special needs, those who are more adjusted to those less adjusted, those who are young (such as babies) to older (such as primary school age and early adolescents in out of school hours care) and those who are able to those who suffer different forms of disabilities. In addition, many early childhood professionals are concerned with the apparent increase in the frequency and intensity of behavioural problems in young children which demand attention.

Today, there is an extensive knowledge about young children and their development compared to previous generations. Both parents and early childhood professionals alike are aware of and understand their roles and responsibilities in nurturing young children's learning and development. The impact and importance of building and enhancing young children's self esteem is a major influence on adult interaction with children, including the ways in which they discipline or manage young children's behaviour.

A number of different approaches to behaviour management typically employed by parents as well as early childhood profes-

1

sionals have been identified by Hoffman (1970). First to be described is the traditional power-assertive approach in which power is asserted over the child by an authority such as an adult or dominant peer. Adults who adopt a power-assertive approach to behaviour management use practices such as physical and verbal punishment and loss of privileges. The disadvantages of a power assertive approach to behaviour management are discussed at length in Chapter 7 and include compliance only in the presence of authority and a tendency to act out when not watched. Another favoured approach, but in fact the least desirable approach to managing young children's behaviour, can be described as love withdrawal where the adult communicates disapproval regarding specific behaviours by withdrawing love, affection, friendliness and warmth. Positive feelings towards a child are replaced by distance, coldness and even active rejection of the child. Adults who use a love withdrawal approach to behaviour management engage in practices such as making negative comments to or about the child, acting in an uninterested, detached, uncaring manner and ignoring the child.

These two traditional ways of responding to children's behaviour are not regarded as acceptable by today's society because of their detrimental effects on young children's development and learning as well as on their self esteem. They also can create long term fear about loss of love as well as anxiety and insecurity about the adult–child relationship in young children.

However, alternative and more acceptable approaches to behaviour management, such as the use of inductive reasoning which is proposed by cognitive-developmental theorists, are available to both parents and professionals who work with children. The inductive reasoning approach to behaviour management which is discussed in Chapters 8 and 9 refers to the use of reasons and explanations in relation to why certain behaviour is considered to be inappropriate as well as providing the answers to the 'whys' concerning limits, rules and requirements. Such an approach helps young children to develop an understanding of and concern for the feelings of others, increases their desire to cooperate based on their understanding of the needs of the situation and helps them to feel secure about becoming a responsible decision maker (Webb, 1989).

Most early childhood professionals put a lot of time and effort into thinking about ways of helping young children to learn to manage their own behaviour more effectively. However, because alternative approaches to behaviour management, such as inductive reasoning, may not be not as familiar as the more traditional methods, some do not consider themselves to be sufficiently skilled in their application and feel uncomfortable when using them. Because early childhood professionals understand that the success of the day to day running of a centre and the quality of young children's learning experiences depend on the way in which children's inappropriate behaviour is managed, they can tend to rely on familiar strategies with predictable outcomes. Consequently, some of the alternative strategies which are available tend not to be employed in the first instance. In addition, some of the alternative approaches appear to take more time to produce results than the traditional methods and therefore may appear less attractive in the short term. It is such concerns, as well as concern with the increasing amount of time which is required to attend to behaviour problems in early childhood centres, which makes this area of such interest.

According to Charles (1992: vi), 'behaviour encompasses all the physical and mental acts that (children) perform . . . good or bad, right or wrong, helpful or useless, productive or wasteful'. It is clear that young children's behaviour encompasses all these characteristics. However, adults who are concerned with the growth, development and learning of young children will observe that much of young children's behaviour does not meet their expectations in relation to being good, right, helpful and productive.

Normal and appropriate behaviour can be considered to be behaviour which does not interfere with the child's ability to cope with the environment and to get along with others. On the other hand, misbehaviour, inappropriate or problem behaviour can be defined as persistent behaviour by children which does not help them fit into, live in and cope with society. It is the kinds of behaviour which act against children's own best interests in the long term and/or indicate a refusal or an inability to learn from the consequences of behaving in a certain way that early childhood professionals need to respond to in order to help young children learn more acceptable ways of behaving.

Herbert (1987) suggested that misbehaviour may be classified into three categories: excesses in behaviour, deficits in behaviour and constellations of behaviour. The usefulness of such a classification is obvious, particularly when supplemented by more specific definitions of misbehaviour such as those proposed by Charles (1992). Charles defined five broad types of inappropriate behaviour which those working in care and education often have to contend with. They are:

- Aggression or any physical or verbal attack by a child on the adults or peers in the centre.
- Immorality or behaviour such as lying and stealing.
- Defiance of authority where children refuse to comply with requests.
- Disruptive behaviour such as talking loudly, pushing in, and throwing things around the room.
- Goofing off which means clowning around, being silly, wasting time and not concentrating on, getting involved in and completing the experiences offered.

The expression of both appropriate and inappropriate behaviour is influenced by the child's personality as well as by family and cultural expectations and differences. Some cultures require that both boys and girls respect their elders and are submissive to adult wishes. Other cultures expect and tolerate the active, individual expressions of behavioural desires from both boys and girls. Certain cultures are more tolerant of and even encourage more dominant and aggressive behaviour from boys while demanding passive and compliant behaviour from girls.

While few early childhood professionals hold unrealistic expectations about what young children are capable of, in terms of controlling their behaviour in accordance with adult expectations there are some occasions when stereotyped ideas about particular children or specific behaviours may influence the early childhood professional's perceptions. Consequently, some early childhood professionals may use inappropriate language when they are referring to young children's behaviour, for example, naughty, disobedient, wicked, bad and rebellious. These terms may reflect ignorance of or a lack of understanding about young children's capabilities and the influences upon their behaviour. Misbehaviour, another common term, refers to behaviour which is regarded to be inappropriate for the situation or context in which it occurs and implies a degree of intentionality. When behaviour unintentionally is inappropriate for a situation or context, it cannot be regarded as misbehaviour because the individual who displayed it may not have known that it was inappropriate or unacceptable. This is the crux of behaviour management. Because they are learning the values, expectations, norms, standards and rules of their culture and society, young children, unknowingly and unwittingly, display a range of behaviours that are not considered to be acceptable. Professionals who work with young children need to be aware of this fact because it underpins the difference between successful and unsuccessful, effective and ineffective approaches to managing young children's behaviour.

Early childhood professionals are very interested in the area of behaviour management because the way in which young children behave and their response to that behaviour can make the day to day running of an early childhood centre harmonious and pleasant or frustrating and unpleasant. Their training means that they understand that babies, toddlers and preschoolers are learning the expectations and rules of their culture and society. Consequently, early childhood professionals, be they preschool teachers, child care workers or family day care providers, have a teaching and guiding role in their professional responsibilities for the care and education of young children.

However, a debate or controversy exists about how best to help young children learn to become socialised members of their culture and society. Each of us tends to hold our own opinions about human nature and how young children are likely to learn how to behave in acceptable ways. For many of us, these opinions will have come from our own experiences as children and how we were socialised or disciplined. Consequently, some early childhood professionals may respond to young children's behaviour with ad hoc, reactive methods which are derived largely from their own personal experience. Few of us will have taken the time to sit down and reflect upon why we do the things we do with children, what the outcomes of our actions are, what we know about young children's development and learning, what we want to and how best we can teach them and what options are available for matching the most effective behaviour management technique with the individual child and the situation. Yet, early childhood professionals regularly engage in these activities in their work with young children and thus need to remember that they will improve their skills and outcomes in behaviour management if they approach it in the knowledgeable, reflective and planned way that they approach other aspects of their roles and responsibilities with young children.

Early childhood professionals are characterised by their nurturing orientation and interest in wanting to do the best thing for young children's development and learning. However, because there are few clear guidelines about what is the most appropriate way to respond to young children's behaviour, some confusion exists about what is the best thing to do or the right way to do it. This confusion begins with the terms that we use to describe young children's behaviour and adult responses to that behaviour. Is a young child's behaviour naughty, bad or wicked? Should the child be punished? Should the behaviour be tolerated? Is it right to discipline young children? Is discipline the same as punishment? What sort of punishment can I use with young children? Is punishment the same as child abuse? If I can't smack a child, what else is left for me? What is self control in young children? While most early childhood professionals believe that young children have the right to be treated with respect, even when they have behaved inappropriately, they need to define behaviour management in terms that are relevant for the early childhood context. This definition will provide some of the answers to the questions above.

DEFINING BEHAVIOUR MANAGEMENT

When early childhood professionals talk about behaviour management, they are referring to the professional responsibility to socialise young children and help them learn to become responsible, competent and fully functioning members of their culture and society according to their developmental capability by using teaching and guidance methods. Such a definition incorporates the concepts of protection, nurturing, encouragement and education which are fundamental to the process of socialisation. The definition also includes the underlying concept of behaviour management as being based on a relationship, that is communication and interaction between adult and child. Young children are socialised more effectively by those adults with whom they have a positive and warm relationship. Indeed, some early childhood professionals, such as those who follow the ideas of Adler and Dreikurs, believe that all inappropriate behaviour is a result of social problems.

Behaviour management can be distinguished from discipline, which in itself has many different connotations. For some people, discipline is equated with compliance, obedience, conformity, suppression, control, coercion and correction of behaviour. While early childhood professionals require compliance with some of their requests in order to create a smooth running program, they do not wish compliance to be at the cost of young children's spontaneity and freedom of expression.

Early childhood professionals would not consider themselves to be successful managers of young children's behaviour if young children blindly obey out of the threat of punishment, suppress their behaviour in the presence of the adult, conform without reason to adult demands, rely on being corrected to produce desired behaviour and behave appropriately through the use of power or superior force! This narrow and negative definition of discipline allies it with punishment which is more concerned with retaliation and retribution for intentional misbehaviour. Windell (1991) lists some of the most punitive and detrimental approaches that have been called 'discipline' by some people. These are physical abuse of or physical attacks on children, physical and verbal coercion, yelling, nagging, demanding immediate compliance, taking anger and frustration out on children, shaming and belittling, setting traps (that is, to catch them being bad) and imposing excessive guilt. Such techniques do not produce children who are able to behave appropriately in a range of settings but tend to lead to increased behavioural and emotional problems later in life. These are certainly not the goals of those who work with young children.

Glasser (1992) suggests that those adults who are concerned with the education of children need to create quality conditions in which fewer adults and children are frustrated from not having their needs met. To achieve this, he recommends that educators adopt the role of 'lead teacher' rather than 'boss teacher' when working with children. Lead teachers develop friendly relationships with children, provide encouragement and stimulation and demonstrate a willingness to support and help them. They 'lead' children into learning experiences that meet their basic needs for:

- Belonging (security, comfort and legitimate membership in the group).

- Power (a sense of significance and being considered worthwhile).
- Fun (enjoying oneself intellectually and emotionally).
- Freedom (to exercise choice, to be self directed and responsible). (Charles, 1992).

On the other hand, boss teachers tend to take a more authoritarian role by dictating the tasks to be completed and defining standards of achievement, dominating the group with their input rather than encouraging input from children and using coercion when children display oppositional or unacceptable behaviour. Lead teachers understand that the motivation for children's learning needs to come from within each child and that the educator's role is to help, in any professional way that they can, children learn. Consequently, lead teachers adopt a problem solving approach to issues of behaviour management. The concept of lead teacher has much relevance for early childhood professionals whose professional responsibilities include stimulating, encouraging, supporting and helping young children learn appropriate behaviour.

Early childhood professionals understand that discipline, while it is a way to control and change behaviour, implies much more. Discipline does have positive aspects when it is regarded as a form of teaching and guidance in order to help children learn (Gordon, 1991). This view of discipline defines its goal as guiding young children's behaviour in ways that encourage socially and culturally appropriate behaviour, develop self control and enhance self esteem. Discipline from this perspective includes helping young children to learn appropriate ways of behaving as well as controlling and changing those behaviours which are considered to be inappropriate without the influence of adult presence. Broadly defined, positive discipline is a process whereby young children learn socially and culturally approved ways of dealing with feelings, interacting with others and of gaining internal, self directed standards of right and wrong.

One aim of many early childhood professionals is for young children to develop self discipline or self control. Both of these terms refer to young children's ability to voluntarily regulate their own behaviour by referring to internalised values, expectations, standards and rules. When young children internalise values, expectations, standards and rules, they adopt for themselves the guidelines that adults have been teaching and helping them learn.

Young children first begin to construct their self concept and second to develop a sense of self esteem out of the evaluation of the self concept. Finally, young children learn self control, that is the regulation of their own behaviour, but this may only be displayed intermittently in children under five years. The development of self control is a slow and gradual process which is an integral part of young children's development and learning in the early years.

The ways in which adults respond to young children's behaviour influences the development of self control. Adults who use positive discipline strategies and authoritative behaviour management approaches foster the development of self control in young children because they appeal to young children's emerging cognitive processes (Pulkkinen, 1982). When children have developed self control, they can control impulses, wait and postpone action, tolerate frustration, postpone immediate gratification and initiate a plan and carry it out over a period of time (Marion, 1991). While infants under two years of age are not developmentally capable of self control, the beginnings of self control emerge at around two years. From then on, young children can take increasing responsibility for their own behaviour.

Behaviour management, while it incorporates the concept of discipline, is much broader because it is based upon the notion that young children's behaviour occurs within specific contexts. Such contexts can help or hinder young children in the expression of inappropriate and appropriate behaviour. Consequently, behaviour management becomes a process of interpersonal interaction which incorporates knowledge about child development, problem prevention, communication and interpersonal relationships, teaching and learning, positive discipline strategies within specific contexts and the development of self control.

SOME BASIC FACTS ABOUT WORKING WITH YOUNG CHILDREN IN EARLY CHILDHOOD CONTEXTS

Managing young children's behaviour effectively does not happen by magic. It is a complex, lengthy, repetitive, difficult and time consuming process. There are few short cuts and there may only be small rewards along the way. This is because young children are gradually learning what is expected from them. They will make many mistakes and they require considerable time, experience and developmental progress to learn to regulate and control their own behaviour. Although managing young children's behaviour can be frustrating for early childhood professionals, the use of positive strategies can lead to more satisfying interaction and relationships between children and adults both of which are fundamental to the work of early childhood professionals.

When responding to young children's behaviour, it is important that early childhood professionals remember the following facts related to working with young children:

1   All children are going to display inappropriate behaviour and engage in misbehaviour at some time or other. It is normal in terms of their development. However, some children will do this more than others. It is naive to assume that merely providing a nurturing environment will foster the development of appropriate behaviour. Even the most friendly and cooperative child will have an off day, as do adults! In addition, many of the experiences that young children seek are legitimate—they are curious and want to learn about the world in which they live. Clewett (1988) argues that it is the responsibility of the early childhood professional to find acceptable ways for young children to gain access to those experiences, not to prohibit them from pursuing those experiences.

2   All children need management or positive discipline. This creates a safe and secure environment where trust, friendship and learning is nurtured. In such an environment, all young children can learn to behave appropriately when they choose to. Many early childhood professionals have witnessed the dramatic change in some children's behaviour according to whether they are home or in an early childhood centre. Even young children can discriminate situations or contexts where certain behaviours are acceptable or inappropriate. The use of effective behaviour management techniques helps children learn what is acceptable and appropriate behaviour for a given setting or circumstance, which in turn helps young children to feel more competent and in control of their lives.

3   Early childhood professionals are unlikely to provide effective care and educational curricula or programs without an effective behaviour management philosophy and program. Caring, educating, teaching and behaviour management are really very similar—they involve processes for bringing about lasting

changes in behaviour. Very little relevant learning can oc in a chaotic environment. Effective behaviour manageme techniques enable early childhood professionals to get on with their main function, that is, caring for and educating young children and fostering their learning.

4   The use of some common and familiar behaviour management techniques can be ineffective and even harmful for young children. For example, reasoning cannot be used with an infant whose needs demand immediate fulfilment, toddlers are not capable physically of waiting for attention, preschoolers do not yet understand abstract notions of right and wrong and some school children are unable to manage their responsibilities and cope with peer pressure.

'Time out' is an example of one commonly used behaviour management strategy which is considered by many professionals who work with young children to be ineffective and sometimes even harmful for dealing with young children's undesirable behaviour. Because early childhood professionals generally are not trained to use this complex strategy, it may be used inappropriately with the result that young children seldom learn anything about why the behaviour that they engaged in was inappropriate. A general description of characteristics associated with the major areas of child development as they pertain to behaviour management is provided in Chapter 2.

5   All early childhood professionals can learn to manage young children's behaviour effectively. Behaviour management is a skill, a procedure, a set of techniques that can be acquired and with practice implemented effectively to produce desired outcomes in children's behaviour. Regular monitoring and evaluation of approaches to behaviour management and outcomes will assist early childhood professionals to refine and become more skilled in their practice.

Early childhood professionals need to develop their own personal system of behaviour management techniques which take the following into account:

1   The realities of the early childhood centre, that is, the physical structure, number of children, number of staff and the atmosphere of the learning environment. Some centres have not been purpose built for group care and education and as such

can create situations which promote inappropriate behaviour in young children, for example, areas where it is difficult for adults to see what is happening. In other centres, the atmosphere between staff may be competitive and elitist with certain staff believing that there is only one way to do things and that is *their* way! Factors such as these need to be considered when developing an approach to managing young children's behaviour.

2   The ages and personalities of the children in the group. Babies, toddlers, preschoolers have different developmental needs and capabilities. Early childhood professionals who are sensitive and responsive to each stage of development will avoid causing problems for themselves which arise from a mismatch between stage of development and behaviour management strategy. Similarly, each child is an individual and brings with her a unique set of characteristics and ways of approaching the world. These factors combine to produce different personalities in children, such as the happy go lucky child, the impulsive child, the tense and difficult child, the outgoing friendly child and the shy, reflective child. Different behaviour management strategies will work better with some children than others and affect their self esteem differently. For example, a look will be shrugged off by one child whereas another child might experience it as humiliating and demeaning. Approaches to behaviour management need to take these factors into account.

3   The professional and personal preferences of the early childhood professional. There are many different theoretical approaches to development and learning which are also relevant for behaviour management—authoritarian and autocratic, permissive and laissez-faire, developmental, authoritative and constructivist. These models have different approaches to and strategies for managing young children's behaviour. Rodd and Holland (1990) summarised the differences between humanistic and behavioural approaches in the early childhood setting. The behaviour management approach selected by an early childhood professional needs to be consistent with her values and professional philosophy which guide other areas of the curriculum or program. In addition, it is pointless selecting an approach to behaviour management which is not consistent with and comfortable as part of one's own personal

style. Trying to be authoritarian if one feels more comfortable with a humanistic orientation will be perceived as false and artificial by young children who may begin to test out the early childhood professional to see where her true orientation lies!

For early childhood professionals, the real challenge of behaviour management is not merely how to manage children's behaviour but rather how to combine the proven elements of a variety of current approaches into a professional but personal style which is:

- Consistent with her own personality and philosophy.
- Effective for the age and behaviour characteristic of the group of children.
- Understood and supported by the parents, other staff and centre administration.
- Easily implemented and a workable system.

Early childhood professionals need to develop a flexible approach to behaviour management which is sensitive and responsive to specific children, specific problems and specific situations. When developing an approach to behaviour management, early childhood professionals should consider how it will impact upon:

- The development of a friendly and trusting relationship.
- The building of self esteem.
- What and how limits are set for children's behaviour.
- The development of communication and social skills in children.
- The encouragement of problem solving and reasoning skills.
- Learning through experiencing the consequences of one's behaviour.
- The development of responsibility, independence and moral autonomy in children.

In conclusion, the time that early childhood professionals take in preparation for, reflecting upon and planning their approach to behaviour management will determine the overall effectiveness of the approach. In the main, most early childhood professionals use their own experience as the basis of behaviour management. In addition, comparatively little training is provided to assist early childhood professionals to understand young children's behaviour and to select appropriate ways of responding to it. The effectiveness of approaches to behaviour management will determine the self confidence, self esteem and job satisfaction experienced by early childhood professionals.

Finally, behaviour management is not something that is put into place on one day or begins when an early childhood professional first has a problem with a child. It is a dynamic process which begins the day a child is born. It is also a fundamental aspect of the early childhood curriculum or program with specific goals. Young children will come to early childhood professionals already having been 'disciplined' by their parents. Although most parents are well intentioned, they may have patchy knowledge about young children, their developmental needs and how best to meet these needs. Some parents will have used poor techniques to control their children's behaviour and it will be a challenge for the early childhood professional to begin anew with these children. Consequently, because children, families and society are continually changing, and because there is no one 'right' way for a given child or situation, approaches to behaviour management need to be continually refined and improved in order to meet young children's rights to and community demands for high quality early childhood services.

2
WHAT IS NORMAL BEHAVIOUR?

Young children's developmental stages

Working with young children becomes much easier when early childhood professionals understand the process of development, young children's developmental limitations and ways to nurture developmental progress. A general understanding of and knowledge about child development will help early childhood professionals who work with children from birth to five years to set realistic expectations, standards and goals in relation to their behaviour. Becoming familiar with ages and stages or developmental levels is one way that early childhood professionals can prevent behavioural problems from occurring, increase their own tolerance of displays of developmentally appropriate but troublesome and irritating behaviours and learn to identify and concentrate on managing inappropriate behaviours which interfere with the provision of an optimum learning environment. This chapter does not provide a comprehensive analysis of child development but aims to draw attention to some of the key developmental issues that impact upon effective behaviour management with children from birth to five years.

The major areas of development are physical, language, intellectual, social, emotional and moral. Factors associated with the first five of these are reviewed in this chapter. Moral development and its relevance to behaviour management is discussed in Chapter 4.

PHYSICAL DEVELOPMENT IN YOUNG CHILDREN

During the early years, young children grow from being physically immature and dependent upon other people to fulfil their needs to becoming physically capable and able to move around in and manipulate their environment. Part of what some adults regard as problem behaviour stems from young children's physical immaturity. Because they are not physically well coordinated and do not have fine motor control, they may bump into things, spill liquids, drop pencils, make a mess when eating their food, be unable to pack away neatly some equipment and materials, fall off outdoor equipment and still may have toileting accidents.

While it may be tempting for early childhood professionals to comment upon young children's lack of physical skill when pouring water or tying up shoe laces and even wish to undertake such activities themselves, young children need opportunities to develop their large and small muscle skills and coordinate their physical abilities. A preventive approach to managing problem behaviours which are a result of physical immaturity is essential. Putting away treasured, breakable objects, providing child sized equipment and furniture, offering realistic activities and experiences and generally child proofing the centre are sensible approaches for responding to behaviour management problems which arise out of young children's physical immaturity.

Another issue associated with young children's stage of physical development is their inability to remain in one place and concentrate for a period of time. Unrealistic expectations about sitting still, being quiet, and spending lengthy periods of time at one activity can be very frustrating for both young children and their carers.

Similarly, young children need sufficient food and rest to ensure that they physically can meet the demands of group care and education. Sensitive early childhood professionals will plan for appropriate snack and meal times as well as quiet rest times for young children. On the other hand, young children also need adequate opportunities to run about, jump, climb and expend some of their energy. Attention to the scheduling of opportunities during the day for gross motor activity also can prevent children from channelling their energy into inappropriate pastimes. Such preventive strategies, which are discussed further in Chapter 6, can avert the need to manage inappropriate behaviours which arise out of young children's physical needs.

LANGUAGE DEVELOPMENT IN YOUNG CHILDREN

Human beings appear to be pre-programmed from birth to be interested in, as well as receptive and responsive to, learning the language that is used in their environment. Although babies do not possess language skills as such, they are determined communicators. Crying is a baby's powerful means for expressing and communicating her needs to the adults around her. Young children, even babies, understand far more language and non-verbal communication cues than they themselves can express. Therefore, it is essential that early childhood professionals talk to and communicate with children of all ages in their care. This helps young children learn to develop and use language skills. It also teaches them that communication is the basis of satisfying interpersonal relationships and a mechanism for solving one's problems. Because discipline and behaviour management are aspects of interpersonal relationships, it is important that young children's language development needs are met.

Infants and toddlers have a growing but limited grasp of receptive and expressive language skills. They can produce pre-speech vocalisations, such as crying and cooing, long before they can produce true speech. Babbling, which occurs about six months of age, is the first sign of an infant's capacity for real language. Unfortunately, many adults confuse the repetition of certain sounds, such as 'ma ma' or 'da da' with an infant's capacity to produce and understand real words, such as 'Mummy' or 'Daddy'. Infants cannot accurately communicate their needs and wishes and rely upon sensitive and responsive early childhood professionals to interpret their rudimentary efforts at communication. The limited language skills possessed by infants and toddlers mean that they are likely to resort to crying and physical means to communicate their wishes. This is not intentional misbehaviour but rather a means to gaining adult attention and responsiveness. So-called behaviour problems, such as displays of anger, pulling away, squirming, crying and throwing objects can arise if early childhood professionals do not respond to an infant's attempts to communicate her needs.

At approximately nine months of age, infants attain the capacity to understand at least some of what is being said to them by adults (Turner and Hamner, 1994), for example, an infant can respond to a simple command and carry out the request. However, infant responsiveness is inconsistent and unpredictable because of developmental limitations. Non-compliance with adult requests should not be interpreted as an intended act of disobedience or defiance.

It is during the first year that infants start to make the connection between language and behaviour. By an infant's first birthday, the child is capable of producing one word sentences which are used to express a complex idea, desire or experience, for example, 'Daddy' which may convey the question 'Is Daddy coming now?', state a fact such as 'Daddy is here now' or express a command such as 'Pick me up Daddy!'. By eighteen months, a toddler has a vocabulary of approximately 25 to 30 words and is starting to put two words together to convey complex meanings. Only key words are used such as 'Me up' or 'Juice gone'. The toddler's ability to understand what is being said to her increases dramatically in the second year. Often, toddlers do not appear to expect anyone to listen to them as they engage in what can be regarded as a continual monologue about their activities. This is called egocentric speech because it does not take into account the perspectives of others. Socialised speech which has a social purpose and takes into account the needs of the listener emerges by three years of age.

Early childhood professionals can facilitate language development in infants and toddlers by talking face to face with them, imitating and responding with smiles, talk or touch to the cooing and babbling of babies and the one and two word sentences of toddlers, talking to them about pictures, daily events and routines, labelling and describing objects and events, playing games and singing songs.

The critical period for language development is between two and four years (Berk, 1991). Most language acquisition to this point is achieved by young children without teaching or correction by adults and it is during this time that their capacity for language develops enormously. By the time children are three, most of them can speak in short, complex sentences and have a vocabulary of approximately 800 words (Turner and Hamner, 1994). By the time young children are five, they have an expressive vocabulary of between 8 000 and 14 000 words and can understand complex communications by adults. It is important to understand, however, that while young children may understand what is being said by an early childhood professional, this may not necessarily have an effect upon the child's behaviour. Many factors operate on a child's decision to modify her behaviour with comprehension being only one of a range of determinants.

It is during the preschool years that young children learn indirectly from exposure to language and without formal teaching the grammar and syntax of their primary language. One of the interesting aspects of preschool language development is the tendency to overgeneralise grammatical rules, such as the rule about making words plural and creating the past tense. For example, the correct plural of words such as toys or cats will be applied to all words, even where it does not apply, such as childrens, mans and sheeps. Similarly, the usual way of forming the English past tense by adding 'ed' to the end of a word may be applied incorrectly to certain words, such as, runned, hurted and sawed. Adult correction of this overgeneralisation of grammatical rules will not help young children adopt the correct form but may act to inhibit children's attempts to communicate. Because most young children will learn to apply grammatical rules correctly by the time they go to school at around five years of age simply through the exposure to language, early childhood professionals should be concerned to attend to the meanings that young children are trying to convey rather than the grammatical correctness of the sentence.

Preschool children are very interested in communicating both with adults and peers and rely on language rather than physical means to express their thoughts and have their needs met. By approximately four years of age, their language indicates that they can be sensitive to the needs of others under certain conditions. Preschoolers understand communication rules and patterns, for example, the need to speak to a listener, the expectation of a response to one's communication and to respond in turn to the listener's response. At this stage, preschoolers can be expected and encouraged to express their desires and resolve their interpersonal problems primarily through the use of language.

Early childhood professionals can facilitate language development in preschoolers using the same strategies suggested for infants and toddlers. In addition, they can assist preschoolers to expand their language competence by providing many opportunities for the use of language skills, acting as language models by using appropriate grammatical forms, introducing a new and expanded vocabulary and by being responsive to preschoolers' questions. They can help young children to extend their language competence by producing complete sentences in response to a child's one or two word sentence. For example, if a preschooler points to the swing and says 'Me swing', the responsive early childhood professional might reply, 'Yes, I see the swing. Would you like a turn on the swing?'

Although young children's capacity with language develops extensively throughout the early years, much refinement will occur during the years of primary and secondary schooling. The early years period is one in which considerable variation is found in the rates at which young children acquire language competence. It is important for early childhood professionals to remember that time and maturation is the basis of language development and that little language is learned by children under five from formal teaching and correction. The most valuable contributions that early childhood professionals can make to young children's language development are first to provide a language-rich environment and second to value and be responsive to young children's increasingly sophisticated attempts at communication.

EMOTIONAL DEVELOPMENT IN YOUNG CHILDREN

Young children come into the world not as blank slates but with a unique combination of inherited characteristics whose development and expression is determined by the people and influences that they experience in their environment. Some children develop personalities which make them easier to get along with and engage in cooperative behaviour while others have personalities which are difficult to manage and seem to be associated with the display of more oppositional behaviour. As well as what they bring as part of themselves to the care and educational setting, young children also go through various stages of emotional development. Emotional development is very relevant to discipline issues because each stage has a particular orientation, task or goal which influences the behaviours that young children engage in (Fields and Boesser, 1994).

Erik Erikson's (1963) theory of the stages of emotional development has been widely accepted by early childhood professionals and is perceived as being helpful for understanding the important influences on young children's behaviours at particular ages and in particular stages. While this theory covers the life span of human beings, only the stages which are pertinent to the behaviour of young children will be discussed here. The stages proposed by Erikson correspond roughly to approximate ages but because individual differences often can be observed in young children, early childhood professionals are advised to use the stages as guidelines regarding expectations about and direction of young children's behaviour.

Basic trust versus mistrust

This orientation, focus or goal of Erikson's first stage of emotional development is the development of babies' and infants' trust or mistrust in the people and world in which they live. Caring adults, such as parents and early childhood professionals, have a responsibility in their relationship with infants to teach them that the world in which they live is a safe and friendly place and that the people who care for them can be trusted to meet their needs promptly, responsively and consistently. If infants learn that they are valued, cared for and respected as significant members of the group, they will have a strong foundation from which to confidently explore and learn about the world as well as for establishing and maintaining relationships. On the other hand, if infants learn from lack of, insensitive or inconsistent adult responsivity to their needs that they are not important in their environment, they may feel insecure, rejected and mistrustful of people and the world. Such infants will not have a secure basis from which to learn and make relationships.

Infants who have developed a sense of trust are more likely to meet adult expectations about behaviour because, at some unconscious and fundamental level, they comprehend that the adults in their world have their best interests and well being at heart. Infants who have developed a basic sense of mistrust become suspicious about their world and the adults in it. Such infants are more likely to act in ways which perpetuate mistrust and consequently result in unsatisfying relationships between adult and child. Unless infants develop a basic sense of trust, they are not psychologically ready or competent to meet the demands of the second stage of emotional development.

Autonomy versus shame and doubt

When an infant enters toddlerhood at approximately twelve to fifteen months of age, the young child's orientation, focus or goal turns to the development of autonomy or independence. The 'easy to get on with' infant appears to change overnight into a power seeking monster! Given their increasing physical and psychological independence from adults, toddlers now wish to see in what ways they can manipulate their world. Toddlers have sufficient self awareness to understand that they are separate individuals with ideas of their own. This stage of development is sometimes known as the 'Terrible Twos' because of toddlers' negativism, desires to exert their will and independence, challenges to adult authority and need to control the situation according to their egocentric perspective.

Sensitive early childhood professionals understand toddlers' needs for choice and decision making opportunities. They are aware that a toddler's need for independence can conflict with her ability to cooperate. They understand that a two year old might even say no when she means yes and are tolerant of toddlers' changes of mind. They provide opportunities for toddlers to cooperate by not demanding compliance with a demand but rather by offering simple alternatives for how the needs of the situation might be met. For example, instead of demanding that the toddler put on gum boots to go outside, a sensitive early childhood professional might ask 'Would you like to put your gum boots on by yourself or shall I help you?'. Similarly, rather than get into a power struggle about whether an apron will or will not be worn for cooking, the early childhood professional could say 'Will you choose an apron for yourself or would you prefer me to choose one for you?'. In this way, toddlers learn that they have some control over their life and what happens to them.

When toddlers are not provided with sufficient opportunities for emotional and physical autonomy, they may develop a sense of shame about their own abilities and struggles for independence as well as doubts about their competence to master the challenges of day to day life. The seeds of poor self concept and low self esteem can be sown during this period by early childhood professionals who do not provide appropriate opportunities for young children to assert their own independence. If children do not feel that they are autonomous and independent beings, they may display developmentally immature and dependent behaviours and will find it difficult to display initiative which is the focus of the third stage.

Initiative versus guilt

While some young children will still be trying to achieve the goals of the previous two stages, those who have had positive experiences during infancy and toddlerhood will be ready to begin to demonstrate initiative. Because preschoolers—that is, three to five year olds—have acquired new developmental capabilities in physical, language and intellectual skills, they are interested in testing and trying out these new found abilities in a range of situations.

Sensitive early childhood professionals will meet the need to show initiative by providing opportunities to contribute meaningfully to the day to day running of the centre by involving young children in discussions about proposed changes, selection of story books and music, the setting of rules, deciding upon appropriate consequences for unacceptable behaviour and problem solving. Young children like to display initiative by participating in and completing meaningful, adult-like tasks such as clearing up, washing up, setting up and packing up. Early childhood professionals need to be willing to hand over some of the control of and responsibility for running the centre to preschoolers to help them take up the challenge of initiative. It is during this stage that preschoolers learn to distinguish between obedience and cooperation.

Lack of opportunity to successfully demonstrate initiative can produce young children who feel guilty about the behaviours in which they engage, particularly if these do not measure up to adult expectations and standards. Where early childhood professionals make acceptance, approval and friendship conditional upon young children's meeting of and compliance with adult expectations, standards and demands, young children can become very insecure, anxious and apprehensive about their relationship with the adult and feel guilty when they cannot meet adult expectations. Young children tend to personalise adult responses to their behaviour, in that they believe that 'it is me who is bad or naughty not what I do'. Early childhood professionals who express disappointment in children, who withhold friendship and who focus upon 'naughtiness' and 'bad behaviour' produce young children who are fearful of showing initiative in case they do the wrong thing and get into trouble or who deliberately engage in unacceptable behaviour as a means of revenge or getting back at the adult who has caused them to feel so demeaned and humiliated. Such preschoolers will not be prepared to move out into and meet the demands of the world of formal schooling in the next stage.

Industry versus inferiority

While most young children are in primary school during this stage of emotional development, it is important for early childhood professionals to be aware of the orientation, focus and goal of this fourth stage. This is a time when five to twelve year olds need to feel that they can independently engage in and complete some of the meaningful tasks which define an individual as a competent, contributing and productive member of their culture and society. It is a stage where young children understand and begin to evaluate their behaviour in terms of success and achievement or failure and inferiority.

Those adults responsible for the care and education of children during this stage, such as those who work in out of school hours and holiday programs, need to understand children's need to be successful and the devastating implications of being labelled a failure. Those children who have developed a positive self concept and self esteem will regard themselves as capable of and interested in meeting adult, cultural and societal expectations. Whereas those who regard themselves as failures may attempt to get even with those believed to be responsible for their lack of achievement by engaging in inappropriate behaviour or withdrawing from situations which might result in further failure. Fewer opportunities to experience success can compound the low sense of self esteem which in turn create a vicious circle for children.

An understanding of the stages of emotional development can assist early childhood professionals with preventing potential behaviour management incidents and alert them to more appropriate and effective intervention strategies should such problems occur.

SOCIAL DEVELOPMENT IN YOUNG CHILDREN

Human beings are social beings. Nearly everything humans do involves other people, affects and is affected by other people. Because new born human infants are highly dependent and require extensive care for a long period of time, it is essential that they develop characteristics and skills which will establish and maintain close relationships with others who are necessary for their survival. While part of the development of social behaviour in young children has a biological basis, much of social behaviour is learned from interacting with other children and adults in the groups in which children spend most of their time. Social immaturity can be the cause of hitting, kicking, biting and grabbing, all of which are behaviour management problems frequently encountered by early childhood professionals. It is important for early childhood professionals to realise that some social problems are a result of developmental immaturity, lack of experience in the social world and young children's perception of the need to compete for limited access to space, resources and adult attention.

For most children, the earliest encounters with others are with their parents in a family environment. It is what children learn about themselves and other people from these earliest social encounters that determines their sense of belonging and their social development. Social development begins very early in life and these early social experiences are considered to lay the foundations for the ways in which children will relate to other people throughout their life.

Parents and significant others, such as early childhood professionals, play a crucial role in influencing children's social behaviour. The main task of parents and early childhood professionals is to socialise young children, beginning at birth, to become socially and culturally acceptable, competent and contributing members of their society. This means that parents and early childhood professionals are charged with the responsibility for helping children acquire the knowledge, behaviours, attitudes, standards and goals that are valued in their society.

In democratic societies, such as Australia, Britain and the United States, parents and early childhood professionals also are expected to socialise children in ways which permit children to gain a sense of themselves as distinct individuals. In these early years, adults have specific responsibilities which change as children grow up. They begin as protectors and nurturers of infants and toddlers but, in addition, must become encouragers and teachers of preschoolers. It is the skills associated with each of these roles that early childhood professionals must learn while they are socialising young children.

The establishment of a positive, warm and loving relationship between parent and child has long been associated with healthy social and emotional development in children. When young children spend many hours in care and educational centres, it is essential that they have the opportunity to develop the same type of relationship with the early childhood professional. Failure to develop such a relationship has been found to have serious negative consequences for children's developmental progress and later interpersonal competence. Therefore, it is important to understand what are the main features of young children's social development and what early childhood professionals can do to enhance or hinder this aspect of development.

Milestones in early social development: birth to two years

In social development, certain challenges are posed to the growing child at specific stages of her life. It is important for early childhood professionals to understand what to expect of children's capabilities at different stages of development in order to work out how best to respond to and meet their needs.

One of the first challenges that an infant faces is to form a secure attachment with at least one adult who will take on the responsibility for ensuring her survival and well being. Infants play an active role in this. Smiling and crying, both of which begin in the first week of life (Bremner, 1994; Davenport, 1994), and responsiveness to the human voice are simple behaviours which help establish and maintain the first relationships, usually with parents. Patterns of social interaction can be noticed by two months of age, with infants rapidly learning ways of prolonging satisfying experiences with parents and early childhood professionals, such as quietening when being held or smiling in response to adults' demonstration of affection or playfulness.

In the first six months, babies learn to express some basic emotions, such as happiness, interest, fear and surprise. They smile and laugh in response to social situations, can imitate the emotional displays of parents and begin to reveal their unique temperamental characteristics.

By twelve months, clear attachment to one significant adult, usually the parent, is present with displays of anxiety in the presence of unfamiliar people (Schaffer, 1990). Early childhood professionals need to provide infants with the opportunity to develop a secure attachment with them as well as to their parents. Infants who are attached to their parents and early childhood professionals feel secure and confident enough to explore their world. They have developed a basic trust which associates the adult with protection from danger. They demonstrate fear of separation if attempts are made to remove them from the proximity of their loved parent or trusted carer.

Early interest in the activities of siblings and peers changes to active play and involvement by eighteen months of age. Children now can recognise themselves in a mirror, photograph or video, have a rudimentary understanding of themselves as an individual, and are capable of complying with some simple requests from parents and early childhood professionals.

By two years of age, children can use language as part of their social interaction, they show sex typed preferences for toys and the beginnings of self control appear.

Later milestones in social development: two to five years

The challenge for children who are around two years of age is to begin to develop a unique sense of self, that is, a self concept and notions of self esteem. This is discussed in detail in Chapter 3. Children develop a self concept and self esteem, sometimes called personal identity, largely from the messages that they receive from the adults around them.

At this age, interest in peers increases, with both cooperative and aggressive behaviours evident. The capacity for self control increases too, although children's behaviour is still largely determined by what is going on around them. Conformity with sex role stereotyped expectations and behaviours are becoming a high priority for boys and girls.

During the third and fourth years, a major challenge is for children to acquire social competence in their relationships with others. This requires that children understand the behaviour of other people and how it might affect their own behaviour. What young children need to learn is the ability to see things from another person's perspective so they are not so self centred. Social cognition, the ability to conceptualise and reason about the social world, influences children's friendships, approaches to conflict resolution and morality.

During this time, the first real friendships are formed with preference for playmates of the same sex. Children can distinguish between social convention (such as, what we usually do in our family) from moral rules (such as, it is wrong to hit someone). Cooperative play with other children increases although aggressive behaviour still is frequent.

Parents and early childhood professionals play a significant role in fostering attachment, self concept, self esteem and social competence in the early years of children's lives. In addition, young children appear to be more compliant and cooperative with adult expectations and requests if they have bonded to and developed a secure attachment to at least one significant person in their life (Honig, 1985; Soderman, 1985).

Bonding and becoming attached

Current ideas about child development suggest that babies are pre-set to develop a close emotional bond with the primary caregivers who are most often, but not always, the mother and father (Campos et al., 1983). For today's generation of children, this may also include the early childhood professional. Research has demonstrated that babies who did not have a significant person to bond to and with whom they could develop a relationship, failed to thrive and had significant delays in all areas of development (Honig, 1985).

Bonding and becoming attached is a process that happens over a number of months. Because babies are not sufficiently cognitively mature to distinguish their mother and father from other adults, they are not selective at first about who meets their needs. The most important issue for the baby is that someone responds promptly and consistently to signals of hunger, discomfort, boredom or the need for physical contact. Gradually, babies develop the perceptual and cognitive skills which enable them to discriminate those who are most sensitive to their needs and who provide the most social stimulation, such as mothers and fathers, from other people that they have contact with, such as professional caregivers.

One factor which is important in the development of attachment is the degree of adult sensitivity or responsiveness to the baby's signals about her needs. It is not sufficient to simply respond to the baby's cues but to be able to recognise the specific need and to meet that need in an appropriate way. If a baby is hungry, picking her up and rocking her will not satisfy her particular need. Most parents and early childhood professionals learn to distinguish a baby's needs from the different types of cries that the baby has. It is this specific responsiveness which is crucial for the development of a basic sense of trust.

Adult responsiveness to a baby's cues may be influenced by the baby's individual personality and temperament. Three broad types of temperament can be seen in newborn infants (Thomas and Chess, 1977):

- Easy babies who tend to be placid, contented, have predictable routines and have a mild response to frustrations.
- Difficult babies who tend to cry a lot, have irregular schedules, are difficult to soothe and who do not adapt well to new situations or people.
- Slow to warm up babies who take time to adjust to but then enjoy new people and situations, react mildly and have somewhat irregular routines.

It is important for early childhood professionals to be aware of their own personality traits and the ways in which they interact with and influence their responsiveness to a baby. A fussy, impatient adult may find dealing with a difficult baby who resists cuddles and attempts to soothe very frustrating. These temperamental traits which are displayed initially in infancy continue to influence behaviour throughout childhood and into adulthood. Soderman (1985) suggests that professionals who work with young children respect individual differences in behaviour associated with temperamental differences, use positive interactions to maintain a friendly relationship and be patient during the lengthy time period involved in young children learning to modify their behaviour.

Adult displays of affection are also necessary for the development of healthy attachment. Cuddling, cooing, rocking, touching, talking, playing games, showing and comforting are some of the important social interactions that will help young children feel securely attached to significant adults. An infant who has at least one secure attachment will be more likely to develop secure relationships with other people in the world, such as grandparents, other familiar adults and children, and care and educational professionals. An infant's relationships with other people, such as early childhood professionals, are not considered to threaten the mother–child bond but rather to contribute to the infant's developing sense of trust in the world and the people in it.

Some parents and early childhood professionals worry that meeting an infant's or young child's needs too soon or too often or giving her too much affection will 'spoil' her. Unfortunately, many parents appear to show the same type and degree of attachment behaviour towards their children as they themselves experienced. Current research suggests that, rather than spoiling infants and young children, prompt, consistent, responsive and timely care is associated with children who have developed a sense of trust, who are happier, more confident and easier to manage when they are older.

When infants have developed bonds and attachments to significant people in their lives and a resultant sense of trust in the world and the people in it, the foundations for developing a positive sense of self, self concept and self esteem have been laid. Those infants who do not become securely attached in the first year are likely to experience problems in later social relationships, may be hostile and socially isolated as children and display behaviours which can be difficult for early childhood professionals to manage.

INTELLECTUAL DEVELOPMENT IN YOUNG CHILDREN

It is important for early childhood professionals to keep in mind that there are enormous differences between the thinking and reasoning capabilities of young children and adults. Young children understand the world from a very different point of view to older children and adults. Consequently, they make interpretations about incidents and their behaviour which are inconsistent from those of the adults involved. The major features of young children's intellectual development are that it is egocentric and dominated by their own perspective. They are cognitively unable to comprehend that others may view the situation differently.

In addition, young children are unable to defer gratification of their needs. They want what they want and they want it now! Consequently, their behaviour appears selfish and inconsiderate with little interest in or regard for other people's feelings or needs. Cognitive immaturity can be the cause of such inappropriate behaviours as telling lies, being selfish, taking things and misunderstanding.

Although modelling may be effective, early childhood professionals cannot teach young children to display more caring and considerate behaviour. Nor does punishment encourage young children to engage in more acceptable behaviour. These skills are dependent upon the stage of their cognitive or intellectual development. Early childhood professionals who understand the development of thinking and reasoning skills in young children can provide an environment which nurtures and fosters these skills.

Jean Piaget's cognitive-developmental theory has thrown much light on how young children's thinking and reasoning abilities differ from those of adults and how they develop over time. Piaget (1971) believed that infants are born predisposed to adapt to and learn from their environment. Infants were considered to be active agents in their own learning, not passive recipients of information from others. Young children were considered to learn from their environment by acting upon it. The action of the individual child enabled that child to gradually construct knowledge about the world. As the individual child constructed knowledge, the two processes of accommodation and assimilation were used to organise the knowledge to fit into existing mental structures. Young children are biologically motivated to gain, expand and refine knowledge about the world and as they do so their mental structures change.

Piaget postulated a six stage theory of cognitive development to describe the qualitative and quantitative changes that occur in the cognitive or intellectual abilities of human beings, with the first two stages relevant for children from birth to five years. Piaget's stage theory and the focus of each stage have been described by Turner and Hamner (1994:19) and modified in the summary below. The first two stages which are relevant to the years from birth to preschool are described in more depth than the final two stages which pertain to primary and secondary school children.

The sensorimotor stage (Birth–2 years)

This is where infants explore their environment and take in information through their senses, process it and act upon it to coordinate sensory input and motor (that is, physical) activities. Piaget believed that this was the basis of knowledge. During this period, infants develop their cognitive capacity from inborn, reflexive actions to explorative skills which allow them to understand the relationship between their own behaviour and its effects upon objects and people. By two years of age, toddlers are capable of intentional and purposeful behaviour and are interested in experimenting and testing out their new found understanding and autonomy. Behavioural expressions of experimentation and testing out are not intentional misbehaviour but rather active efforts to discover and learn about the world.

The pre-operational stage (2–7 years)

This consists of two sub-stages in which major shifts in young children's thinking can be seen. The first sub-stage is called pre-conceptual and covers the age period of approximately two to four years. The young child demonstrates a limited but increasing ability to use symbolic functioning which is evidenced by language, pretend play and drawing. Because no true concepts are formed, it is called pre-conceptual. The child's ability to reason and think logically is restricted in this stage and it cannot be taught by adults. Only maturity and the opportunity to interact with the environment will produce the ability to reason and think logically.

The pre-conceptual stage is characterised by egocentrism which means that the child's thinking is dominated by her own perspective. The young child is cognitively unable to take into account the perspective of other people concerning a situation or event. This is why young children often appear selfish and inconsiderate. However, early childhood professionals need to recognise that this is not an instance of unacceptable behaviour but behaviour which is a product of cognitive immaturity. Further cognitive development which entails a decline in egocentrism rather than correction is what is needed for socially acceptable behaviour to emerge.

The second stage in the pre-operational period is called the intuitive stage and covers the ages of approximately four to seven years. Young children in the intuitive stage cannot think by operations yet but can form mental representations of objects and events and are able to manipulate and transform information in rudimentary ways. Children in this stage attain classification, conservation and serial/ordinal understanding and skill. Yet their thinking is dominated by intuitions, which means that they make guesses about reality which are often wrong from an adult perspective.

One characteristic of intuitive thinking is the inability of young children to separate fantasy from reality. This is why some young children have imaginary playmates, 'tell lies' or make up stories about their life. This confusion between fantasy and reality is again a sign of cognitive immaturity. Reprimanding or correcting young children for their flights of fantasy is an inappropriate response to what is part of the normal development of young children.

Although egocentrism begins to decline slowly during the intuitive period, young children's thinking is still dominated by their own perspective, needs and desires. While young children may be able to take the perspective of another when talking about a hypothetical character or event, powerful cues in the immediate context mean that they are often unable to apply that skill to situations or events in which they are personally involved (Rodd, 1988). In reality, young children's thinking is considerably rigid during the preschool years which means that they can appear to have some understanding about a situation, yet act irrationally when presented with a concrete incident.

The concrete operations stage (7–11 years)

This is when children gradually exhibit the ability to understand the logical principles that apply to concrete, external objects. Children can form true concepts, are less egocentric, can reverse operations, understand cause and effect and are more flexible in their thinking and reasoning.

The formal operations stage (11 plus years)

This is attained through early adolescence where children develop the capacity to think much like adults. Their thinking demonstrates the ability to think abstractly within the constraints of the immediate situation and to think in terms of possibilities and probabilities. Although children in this stage may have developed the capacity for flexible, adult-type thinking, they may not use these skills consistently or predictably for some time and evidence of regression to earlier forms of thinking can be found.

Although later theorists have pointed out the limitations of Piaget's theory of cognitive development, most early childhood professionals will have observed the characteristics of young children's thinking in their day to day interaction with young children. One of Piaget's contributions to adult understanding of young children is the fact that young children think differently about the world to adults and that their cognitive immaturity is a factor which needs to be taken into account when interpreting the meaning of their behaviour. When early childhood professionals understand cognitive development and its relationship to behaviour management, they will consider how a particular child thinks, whether the child can understand what the adult is saying and whether the child can take into account another person's perspective when deciding how best to respond to a behavioural incident.

The theoretical contribution of a Russian psychologist called Vygotsky has provided an alternative perspective to that of Piaget about cognitive development and its implications for adults' roles in relation to young children's learning. Vygotsky's ideas have been gaining increasing interest from and acceptance by members of the early childhood profession. Vygotsky (1962, 1978) took a socio-cultural perspective and believed that children's intellectual development had its origins in social contexts. Whereas Piaget considered children to be 'natural scientists' who learn by investigating their world, Vygotsky argued that the social and cultural context had a marked impact on children's thinking. Piaget believed that development preceded and drove learning. Vygotsky, on the other hand, believed that good learning preceded and drove development. Consequently, he argued that teaching should precede children's development levels because teaching stimulated the maturation of children's cognitive functions. Young children moved to higher developmental levels when they were stimulated and guided at the outside of their limits by sensitive adults.

Vygotsky viewed child development as a result of young children's competence being challenged and extended with help from others, both adults and peers. The development of thinking was considered to be a shared endeavour between adults and children rather than an individual process for each child (Smith, 1993). When adults provide guidance and interactional support in 'the zone of proximal development', young children exhibit greater competence in their thinking. The 'zone of proximal development' refers to the gap between the actual level of development which is determined by individual problem solving and the level of potential development which is determined by problem solving shared between the adult and child, under adult guidance and support and in collaboration with peers. Vygotsky used the metaphor 'scaffolding' to describe the interactional guidance and support that responsive adults offer young children and their intellectual efforts. Sensitive adults gradually withdraw their help as children become able to think and do more and more on their own. Vygotsky believed that what children learn and can do today with assistance and guidance, they can do tomorrow alone, unaided and independently. Consequently, from Vygotsky's perspective, the role of the adult in the development of young children's thinking is critical.

Vygotsky also believed that language was central to young children's development, with speech being an essential tool to permit children to plan and carry out action, deal with incidents and events and control their own behaviour. Through the use of language, children's thinking is developed. The implications for managing young children's behaviour are self-evident.

From a Vygotskian point of view, early childhood professionals can facilitate learning, and from that development, by becoming sensitive social partners who are aware of what young children can do and understand. Early childhood professionals need to become 'warm demanders' of young children's cognitive development and thinking (Meade, 1995) by creating a caring and warm relationship. This will assist them to share young children's frames of reference so that they can provide the extensive 'scaffolding' that young children initially require for learning and development to occur. Early childhood professionals can effect good educational outcomes for young children by being warm, capturing the 'teachable moment' and engaging in challenging practices.

The most important thing for early childhood professionals to understand about young children's cognitive development is that it cannot be formally taught, rushed or hurried. Young children gain cognitive maturity by interacting with the social world and acting upon the physical world. Early childhood professionals can facilitate young children's cognitive development and learning by providing a child-focused, play-oriented, developmental curriculum or program. This does not mean standing back from children's thinking and missing the 'unreturnable moment' (Meade, 1995). Rather than acting as a formal instructor, sensitive early childhood professionals will regard themselves as 'warm demanders' who prepare an environment and interact with young children in ways which will provide opportunities for and challenge young children to develop and extend their intellectual abilities.

In conclusion, early childhood professionals need to keep in mind that high quality services and programs promote all areas of the child's development and apply knowledge of child development to curriculum and program practice (Bredekamp, 1987). Sensitive early childhood professionals will ensure that they have a comprehensive understanding of child development in order to identify what kinds of behaviours are regarded as normal and to be expected at certain ages and stages. Such knowledge can help early childhood professionals distinguish between behaviour that is a function of developmental immaturity and behaviour which is purposeful misbehaviour or unintentionally inappropriate. This information can help early childhood professionals select behaviour management strategies which are more likely to be effective in eliminating undesirable behaviour and gaining more appropriate behaviour from young children.

3

BEING GOOD
AND FEELING GOOD
ABOUT IT

Fostering young children's
self esteem

The attitudes and behaviour of the people with whom young children interact, including early childhood professionals, have a marked effect upon young children's self esteem. A significant collection of research evidence points to the fact that young children who feel secure within the group do not usually engage in more than normal and developmentally appropriate misbehaviour, that is, they do not cause too much trouble (Charles, 1992). Young children who develop a positive self concept and a high sense of self esteem show a willingness to cooperate and engage in independent and responsible behaviour. Early childhood professionals have a responsibility to interact with young children in ways which strengthen young children's self concept and self esteem. If early childhood professionals only acted as agents of intervention in managing young children's behaviour, this would ensure that young children would continue to engage in unacceptable behaviour and not learn socially and culturally acceptable ways of behaving. The detrimental effects of punishment on young children's self concept and self esteem are discussed in Chapter 7.

When self concept and self esteem are enhanced, young children are provided with an atmosphere which is optimum for learning appropriate behaviour while at the same time reducing inappropriate behaviour. Raising young children's self concept and self esteem is a preventive approach for reducing and eliminating unacceptable behaviour. It is essential for early childhood professionals to understand the nature and role of self concept and self esteem in discipline and the management of young children's behaviour. Biddulph (1994) is an excellent resource for early childhood professionals who wish to explore further the impact of self concept and self esteem on young children's behaviour.

SELF CONCEPT AND ITS DEVELOPMENT

The self is a cognitive construct that a person builds about themselves and which gradually develops over time. It is a view or understanding about oneself that grows as a result of experience with the world and the people in it. Part of self concept is self knowledge, such as the knowledge that each one of us is a separate entity and that each of us has a specific gender which is constant (Marion, 1991). For both adults and children, their understandings and ideas about themselves influences their behaviour, in that behaviour tends to be consistent in relation to the knowledge each of us holds about ourselves. For example, a child who knows that she is a girl is likely to engage in girl-type behaviour and not choose to and perhaps actively resist engaging in behaviour that she considers to be boy-like. In the same way, a young boy may refuse to wear clothes that he considers to be girl-like, such as a pink tee shirt, socks with pastel flowers on them or tights! Similarly, a girl may spontaneously display helping behaviour, such as clearing dishes and washing up whereas a boy is more likely to walk away from such situations or be unwilling to engage in such activity because it does not fit in with his knowledge about himself as a boy and his stereotyped notions concerning what boys do!

The development of the self is dynamic, that is, all of us continue to gain knowledge, views and understandings about our selves over time. For young children, they are interested in and collect information about their physical appearance (for example, I am tall, I am short, I have a big nose, I am pretty, I am fat, I have red hair, I wear glasses, I have brown skin), physical abilities (I can run fast, I can balance on the board, I can't jump rope, I can't turn off a tap, I can do my shoes up), their gender (I am a girl, I am a boy), their intellectual abilities (I am slow, I am clever, I can write my name, I can put puzzles together quickly, I don't know the answers to many questions, I can't remember the songs), and interpersonal skills (I belong to the group, I fit in, I cannot get the other children to play with me, I have a lot of fights, I know how to get my own way, I can tell people what I want).

Young children also develop understandings about themselves in relation to their behaviour. They may regard themselves as attractive, popular and competent or unattractive, not liked and incompetent. Such views are likely to influence their behaviour, in that children who have a positive self concept tend to act in accordance with this knowledge and are less likely to engage in unacceptable behaviour, whereas children with a poor self concept see themselves as not fitting in or meeting expectations and are more likely to behave in a way that fulfils this belief. It is therefore in the best interests of both young children and early childhood professionals to communicate and interact with young children in ways that facilitate the development of a positive self concept.

Marshall (1989) offers a range of strategies for early childhood professionals to use in order to influence the development of positive self concept in young children. These are outlined below.

1 Help children feel they are of value by:
- Listening attentively to what young children say.
- Asking for their suggestions.
- Helping them to identify their own positive and prosocial behaviours.
- Highlighting the value of different cultural and ethnic groups.

2 Help children learn interpersonal skills by:
- Teaching skills for positive social interactions with peers.
- Teaching language for expressing wishes and feelings.
- Assisting them with conflict resolution strategies.

3 Become aware of your own expectations for children by:
- Being open to new information about children and looking at them in new ways.
- Being aware of whether your expectations are influenced by gender bias, that is, having different expectations for girls and boys.

4 Help children develop a positive sense of self esteem by:

- Encouraging them to feel that they are competent, have some control.
- Helping them to learn to realistically evaluate their own accomplishments.

Strategies for helping children to develop self esteem will be discussed in the next section.

SELF ESTEEM AND ITS DEVELOPMENT

Once young children have accumulated some knowledge and understanding about who they are, that is, a self concept, they begin to evaluate this information and decide whether they are happy with who and what they are, that is, whether their self concept meets with their approval or disapproval. Marion (1991:209) describes this as the child 'evaluates and forms an opinion about the self that he sees'. Self esteem then is the evaluative part of the self, a subjective, personal judgement of worthiness. Such judgements can be favourable and positive in which case a high level of self esteem is developed. Alternatively, they can be unfavourable and negative from which a low level of self esteem grows.

Self esteem in young children develops largely because of the attitudes towards them of the adults who are important in the lives of young children. Significant adults, such as the early childhood professional, feed information to the child telling her what the adult's attitude is towards the child. If early childhood professionals set artificial, superficial or unreasonable standards and expectations for young children, such as beauty, cuteness, levels of intelligence or physical prowess, they may set children up automatically for failure and the development of feelings of inferiority. Young children may believe that they may never be able to measure up to such standards and consequently experience feelings of self doubt. Low self esteem in young children can be a result of adult attitudes and behaviour which degrades, demeans, humiliates or rejects them. On the other hand, high self esteem in young children is produced from adult behaviour which communicates acceptance, attention, support, encouragement and affirmation.

DIMENSIONS OF SELF ESTEEM

Given that self esteem has such a marked influence on whether young children engage in acceptable or unacceptable behaviour, one of the critical ways of increasing appropriate behaviour and decreasing inappropriate behaviour is to raise their self esteem. There are three major building blocks of self esteem which include competence, control and worth (significance to others). As with other areas related to self, young children form attitudes about their ability to be competent, to be in control and to be regarded as worthy and significant. It is important that early childhood professionals be aware of these dimensions and interact in ways which assist young children to develop positive attitudes about themselves and skill in each of them.

Competence

Helping young children to feel that they are capable of and competent to meet the demands of their environment is an important task for early childhood professionals. Young children are still learning about adult expectations and standards and they are developing in physical, language, intellectual, social, emotional and moral ability. However, they are constrained by developmental limitations and early childhood professionals need to ensure that young children are provided with training and sufficient opportunities and time for learning as well as support and assistance in order to meet the demands for achievement that are placed upon them.

As with adults, young children's behaviour is motivated by the need to feel competent and successful. Young children inherently enjoy mastering something new and becoming more independent. In addition, they require adult attention and approval to realistically affirm their competence and mastery. It can take quite a deal of skill from early childhood professionals to provide young children with realistic and affirming feedback about their performance. Such feedback needs to be related to reasonable standards and expectations as well as to individual developmental capacity. Children may need assistance from the early childhood professional to set realistic and reasonable goals for themselves. Some children have a tendency to overestimate their ability to achieve while other children may underestimate their ability to be successful in a given situation. Both of these tendencies can diminish a young child's sense of competence. Even very young children know when they easily accomplished a task and do not respect exaggerated positive feedback. Failure to be successful is a common source of low self esteem!

Both Albert (1989) and Marshall (1989) offer early childhood professionals a number of strategies which can help children feel capable and competent:

1   Teach young children to believe in their ability to master a certain skill or task by raising their 'I can' level. If a young child believes 'I can' as opposed to 'I can't', they feel good about themselves which in itself creates an emotional atmosphere conducive to mastery and success. It is important that the 'I can' level be set in relation to their level of development.

2   Provide experiences for children where they can succeed by relating the activity to something that they have already mastered, are familiar with and can recognise. Similarly, break a big task down into a number of smaller, simpler steps which gradually increase in difficulty.

3   Teach strategies for and allow opportunities for accomplishing tasks. Remember 'I can't' may mean 'I don't know how'.

4   Allow children to carry out and complete the tasks by themselves even if it is going to take more time than if an adult completed it for or assisted the child with the task.

5   Permit the child to make mistakes and communicate the message that mistakes are okay. Help young children understand that making mistakes is part of the learning process and that all children and adults make mistakes! Turn the mistake into a learning opportunity by talking about what could have been done differently next time. Avoid being 'mistake oriented' by not commenting on every error or mistake. Focus on helping young children overcome one or two mistakes at a time.

6   Build children's confidence by giving positive feedback which focuses on improvement, notices contribution, builds on strengths, communicates faith in their abilities to meet expectations and acknowledges the difficulty of a task. It may also be helpful to set time limits on tasks so that young children do not think that something which they find difficult is going to go on for a long time.

7   Provide new challenges and comment on positive attempts to master the task. It may also be helpful to focus on and repeat past successes in order to encourage young children's belief in themselves.

8   Recognise young children's achievements in tangible ways and by teaching them self approval, that is, to recognise and talk about what they did well. This prevents young children becoming dependent on external approval from either peers or adults.

Control

Young children need to feel that they have some degree of control or power over their lives. Early childhood professionals want to encourage young children to be independent, responsible and involved with the group. One way of achieving this is to help young children feel that they are responsible for the outcomes of their behaviour. Rather than considering themselves to be victims of circumstances, with young children attributing or blaming the consequences of their behaviour on outside influences, luck or events beyond their control, they need to learn that it is their choice and effort that influence whether or not they achieve a goal.

Marshall (1989) suggests the following strategies for enhancing young children's sense of control:

1   Provide opportunities for choice, initiative and autonomy. Never do for children what they can do themselves. Offer simple and limited choices. Ensure that the curriculum or program includes a range of tasks at different levels of difficulty.

2   Avoid competition and comparison between children. Most young children do not understand and cannot cope with competition (Fields and Boesser, 1994). Competition is very destructive for young children's self esteem because there is usually only one winner. The other children become discouraged about their efforts because they are not considered to be the best. Some will want to withdraw while others will begin to engage in destructive activities to help themselves come out on top or to prevent there being any winner at all, such as destroying other children's work, sabotaging games and bullying children out of the activity. In the same way,

comparison is also destructive because it focuses on one child's strengths and the other child's deficiencies. It is important for early childhood professionals to encourage and support each child's activities independently. The work of Dreikurs and Dinkmeyer and their colleagues is important in understanding how to avoid comparison and competition and is discussed further in Chapter 9.

3   Help children learn to evaluate their own accomplishments. Instead of comparing their performance to that of others, sensitive early childhood professionals will teach children to evaluate their own performance by talking about improvement from an earlier attempt, the results of practice and effort on performance, and asking children to talk about what they liked about what they did. In this way, young children are freed from being dependent on external adult evaluation and approval.

Worth and significance

In order to feel good about themselves, young children need to feel that they are of value. This refers to their belief about the extent to which they like themselves, perceive themselves to be liked by their peers and the early childhood professionals with whom they spend their day and whether they consider themselves to be accepted by others and deserving of attention (Marion, 1991). Young children who believe that they are competent, likeable, accepted, generally able to meet adult expectations and worthy of attention tend to develop high and positive levels of self esteem and confidence whereas those who consider themselves to be incompetent, unlikeable, unaccepted or rejected, often unable to meet adult expectations and unworthy of attention are likely to have low and negative levels of self esteem. To help young children feel of value, it is recommended that early childhood professionals use the strategies that Marshall (1989) suggested for influencing self concept which are outlined earlier in this chapter. What is essential is that early childhood professionals communicate opinions and attitudes and behave towards the child in ways which let the child know that she is valued. Young children tune in to the early childhood professional's verbal and non-verbal messages and create or modify their own attitude towards themselves to match those of the adults.

In addition to competence, control and worth or significance, Albert (1989) suggests that there are two other building blocks which underpin young children's self esteem. These are opportunities to help young children connect to and find a place in the group and opportunities to contribute to the group.

Connection

Albert (1989) argues that adults assist young children to connect and find a place in the groups to which they belong by forming relationships with them. This is a special relationship which involves acceptance, attention, appreciation, affirmation and affection. Albert suggests that adults who model such attributes teach young children to 'initiate and maintain positive relationships with their peers . . . be receptive to (adult) efforts to discipline, to instruct or to help in other ways' (p.117).

Acceptance is communicated by accepting the doer, not the deed, and accepting children's personal idiosyncrasies in dress and habits.

Attention is communicated by greeting children by name, listening attentively and responsively to them, giving non-verbal signals that display interest and spending time with them on a one to one basis.

Appreciation is communicated by appreciating the deed not the doer, focusing on the present and giving positive verbal, written and non-verbal feedback.

Affirmation is communicated by identifying and commenting upon young children's desirable, acceptable and appropriate characteristics and behaviours.

Affection is communicated by verbal and non-verbal expressions of friendship and intimacy, such as empathy, kindness, compassion and touch.

Young children's opportunities to form positive relationships, connect with and find a place in the group are reduced if early childhood professionals spoil the child by overlooking and not responding to inappropriate behaviour, by doing too many things for young children which they could have done themselves and by intervening in and not permitting them to experience the consequences of situations created by themselves and other young children.

Contribution

In managing young children's behaviour, some important long term goals are to help them learn to become responsible, empathic and contributing members of the group. When young children learn that the behaviour which they choose to engage in can affect the well-being of their peers, they are beginning to learn that how they behave and contribute to the group is linked to the overall emotional atmosphere and smooth running of the early childhood centre. Giving young children the opportunity to contribute in meaningful ways helps them to feel needed, to belong, to feel competent and capable and influences the development of a positive self concept and high self esteem.

Young children can contribute to the group by being included in decision making about the curriculum, program and rules, being asked their opinions and preferences and by participating in routine and regular tasks which need to be undertaken daily. In addition, young children can be provided with opportunities to help one another in learning and social situations. This raises self esteem and can also create a special bond between children. Encouraging young children to recognise and acknowledge the contributions of other children in the group is also valuable.

GUIDELINES FOR DEVELOPING SELF CONCEPT AND SELF ESTEEM

In the previous sections, specific strategies for influencing self concept and self esteem have been outlined. To act in an accepting and supportive way overall, early childhood professionals need to monitor their own behaviour and follow the following guidelines which have been adapted from Marion (1991).

1   Respect the child as a person and value her for who she is, not what she does. Act towards young children in ways that you would expect others to act towards you.
2   Be reasonable in your expectations for good behaviour. Learn what is reasonable for each stage of development. Develop fair and reasonable limits which are stated clearly and firmly enforced.
3   Be patient. A young child may not know which of your requests are important and may test you to find out. Make sure that young children understand what you expect of them.

4   Require young children to be autonomous and to take respon-
    sibility for their own behaviour. Don't underestimate young
    children's ability to handle situations.
5   Encourage young children to take credit for doing something
    well and not to dwell on their deficiencies. Be sensitive to
    their feelings of self worth and avoid constantly pointing out
    what the child has done incorrectly.
6   Acknowledge and help young children work through their
    feelings such as frustration, anger, jealousy and envy.
7   Show genuine interest in and enthusiasm for young children's
    interests and appropriate activities. Engage in joint activities
    willingly and positively.
8   Avoid stereotyping young children on the basis of age, gender,
    culture or personal attributes.
9   Use positive behaviour management techniques. These are
    outlined in Chapter 9.

In conclusion, when early childhood professionals understand the
link between young children's positive self concepts, high levels
of self esteem and appropriate behaviour, they understand the
need for engaging in teaching and behaviour management practices which promote the positive development of these aspects of
development. When young children are motivated to engage in
appropriate behaviour, early childhood professionals feel better
about themselves, that is, their own sense of self esteem is raised
and anecdotal evidence suggests that they report greater job
satisfaction. They appear to be freed from the need to criticise,
to embarrass, to nag and to threaten young children, all of which
diminish young children's feelings about themselves and their
desire to cooperate in the early childhood centre. Strengthening
self concept and self esteem is an interpersonal component of
behaviour management and is based on the personal attitudes and
behaviour of the early childhood professionals, a curriculum or
program that provides for young children's genuine success, young
children's understanding of the purposes of and reasons behind
behavioural expectations and a sense of togetherness in the group
for meeting the demands of daily living.

4

WHEN DO CHILDREN UNDERSTAND RIGHT AND WRONG?

Moral development in young children

Many parents and early childhood professionals ask the questions 'Can we teach children to be good?' and 'What can I do to ensure that my child learns to behave appropriately?'. Adults today also express concerns about a perceived general decline in such things as respect for authority, politeness and good manners. They are concerned about rude and aggressive children, bad language and offensive attitudes. Many parents and early childhood professionals regard our more permissive society as producing undisciplined children, many of whom appear to grow into anti-social teenagers.

While anecdotal evidence and our own unsystematic observation might accept this point of view, it is important not to approach moral development without carefully questioning the status quo and rationally considering the assumptions we make about the apparently undesirable situation that exists among children. Early childhood professionals need to reflect upon where they stand on moral issues. An understanding of philosophy is helpful for examining existing expectations, beliefs and values in order to clarify the concepts that are used as a basis of statements, arguments and justifications about the role early childhood professionals adopt in relation to young children's moral development and education. However, it is also necessary to understand the precise characteristics of moral behaviour and understanding that can be reasonably expected from young children, what factors are associated with the development of moral understanding and conduct, including prosocial behaviour and, finally, what strategies may be useful for parents and early childhood professionals to facilitate moral understanding and behaviour in young children. Decisions about how to discipline and teach young children how to cope in the world should be based on an understanding of the development of morality (Stengel, 1982).

MORAL DEVELOPMENT AND SOCIAL COMPETENCE

To become a socially competent member of society, children need to understand that a range of social rules exist which govern social interaction in different social settings. Parents and significant others in children's lives have a responsibility to teach such rules. Children need to learn rules that are related to:

- Moral issues, such as it is wrong to hit other people, it is wrong to tell lies and it is wrong to destroy other people's property.
- Social conventions, such as you need to wear a smock when you are painting, use a fork rather than your fingers and we put shoes on to go outside.
- Safety matters, such as we walk inside, no splashing or grabbing in the pool, we wash our hands after going to the toilet and we need to wear sun cream and a hat when we are outside.

Children are exposed to a variety of social rules and expectations in different settings and quickly understand that rules which apply in one setting do not necessarily apply in another setting. For example, children soon learn that it might be acceptable to put your feet up on the sofa at home but that it is not acceptable at Grandma's. They learn that at an early childhood centre it is expected that you pack up when you have finished playing with the blocks but that at home this rule may not be enforced consistently. Preschool children understand that it is okay to use certain words with your friends but that these words are taboo at creche or in front of some, but not necessarily all, adults! Children of this age also understand that there are some rules that do not change regardless of the circumstances, such as it is wrong to kill, it is wrong to hurt others and it is wrong to steal.

Children's earliest encounters with social rules occur in the context of the family. Early childhood professionals need to be aware that young children have a limited understanding of these rules and that this understanding develops over time. For example, children do not fully understand the concepts of right and wrong until they are in primary school. Neither do they comprehend the complexities of 'fairness' from an adult point of view. Rather, they perceive situations and events from their own perspective. Between five and nine years of age, children come to understand the difference between accidental and intentional behaviour and the implications for the consequences of that behaviour.

While young children may be able to 'mouth' or recite a rule, this does not necessarily mean that they can apply the rule when confronted with a choice in a specific situation (Artmann, 1979). This can be confusing for early childhood professionals who think that if a child can tell you that she may not splash water during water play, then the child should be able to control the desire to break the rule and keep the water in the trough. However, young children's responses to the here and now are strongly influenced by the concrete cues in the situation (such as the physical feel of the water) not a tiny voice in their head (such as the early childhood professional reminding them about the rule)!

Adults can assist young children to become socially competent, that is, to be aware of what sort of behaviour is both socially and culturally appropriate in a range of situations, by setting and communicating clear rules about social behaviour. For example, letting children know that it is acceptable to swim in the wading pool at home without wearing a swimsuit but that a swimsuit will need to be worn at the early childhood centre or local pool.

To help young children understand the impact of their behaviour upon other people, it is important that the early childhood professional point out how the other person might be feeling. For example, if a child grabs a toy from another child, it is helpful to say something like 'John is upset because you took his truck without asking him. How would you feel if someone did that to you?'. Asking the child for her ideas about how she might respond to another child's distress (for example, 'How could you help John feel happy again?') assists children to identify possible options to resolve such interpersonal conflicts. Many of the interpersonal issues that young children face are moral ones (Alper, 1989). Therefore, early childhood professionals need to understand what morality is, how it develops and their role in facilitating young children's moral understanding and behaviour.

UNDERSTANDING MORALITY

There are a number of general concepts related to moral development in young children (that is, the development of an understanding of society's rules and of what is right and wrong), which are important for early childhood professionals to understand. These are summarised in the following points.

1   All cultures consider that it is a basic task and responsibility of the adults who are responsible for children to teach children moral standards and rules. These rules are important for human interaction and relationships in society.

2   While most cultures regard children's understanding of and capacity for moral conduct as different to that of adults, most consider that it is important for children to develop a sense of moral autonomy, in which children move from being reliant on external sources of power, such as authority figures, to guiding and regulating their own behaviour by reference to an internalised system of rules (Kamii, 1984).

3   Since morality is so important in human behaviour and interaction, many theorists have proposed explanations about what morality consists of and how it develops in children. It is interesting to note that morality is not a simple construct. Consequently, not one theoretical perspective adequately explains morality and its development. Basically, morality is made up of three relatively independent aspects, behavioural, affective and cognitive, each of which is explained by different theoretical perspectives. It is necessary to become familiar with the three components of morality and their theoretical explanations in order to develop an integrated understanding of moral development. Unfortunately, little consistency can be observed between what people know, think and believe, what they feel about potential behaviour and actual behaviour, and what they do when confronted with a moral dilemma.

The three aspects of morality and their theoretical bases are defined as:

- *The behavioural aspect*, which refers to actual behaviour or conduct in moral situations. Here, moral behaviour is explained by learning theory which includes the effects of reward, punishment, observation and modelling.

- *The affective aspect*, which refers to the emotions, feelings of guilt or satisfaction derived from thought and behaviour in moral situations. These are explained by psychoanalytic theory and include the development of the conscience.
- *The cognitive aspect*, which refers to the knowledge of moral rules, judgements of good and bad, the capacity to understand rules and which is explained by cognitive-developmental theory.

4   There are many different definitions of morality which describe children who are supposedly morally mature. In many cases, such definitions refer to 'socially aware children'. Social awareness includes being able to share, show self-control, care for property and the environment, show empathy, understand that one's behaviour affects others and take intentions into account as well as having a positive self concept (Goodall et al., 1983 in Straughan, 1991). Straughan (1991) argues that such definitions do not describe morally mature children but are prescribing what such children ought to be. He goes on to state that a socially aware child is one 'who is aware of and has some understanding of social forces, factors and conditions . . . that human beings interact in various interesting ways and do not operate as individuals' (1991:25). These children may be aware but, in fact, might also be selfish, intolerant, greedy and unsympathetic.

Straughan (1991:29) describes a number of claims that adults who live and work with children have been found to make in relation to children's moral development. His statements (with names modified) illustrate a range of understanding and definitions of what children's morality and 'being good' is all about:

- Jane is a good girl. She always does what she is told.
- Gian is a good boy. He never argues or answers back.
- Nasreen is a good girl. She is always ready to help anyone in trouble.
- Jonathan is a good boy. He's always so worried if he feels he's done anything wrong.
- Eleni is a good girl. She never misses a Sunday School class.
- Jason is a good boy. He's never been in trouble with the police.

- Yasmin is a good girl. She never skips her homework.
- Tomas is a good boy. He's always so upset if anyone is unhappy.
- Gisela is a good girl. She always does what is right without having to think about it.
- Spiros is a good boy. He means well—though he often gets led astray.
- Janine is a good girl. If she believes she needs to do something, she'll not rest until it's done.

All of the above statements reflect different perceptions and definitions that adults hold in relation to 'morality' for young children. It is important for early childhood professionals to reflect upon their own definition of morality and use it as a reference point when evaluating young children's behaviour. One definition of morality that is relevant for early childhood professionals is that morality is 'a set of rules, customs or principles which act as guidelines to regulate people's conduct in relation to other people and which children (and adults) can use to judge their own actions and the actions of others'.

5   In addition to different aspects and definitions of morality, different levels or types of morality also can be identified. These are:

- *Primitive morality*, which is a pre-rational, group enforced morality where conformity to rules is ensured out of fear of punishment or consequences
- *Intermediate morality*, which is an internalised morality characterised by an irrational acceptance and internalisation of society's moral values and standards, rather than an acceptance through rational examination of rules and standards.
- *Mature morality*, which is a personal, rational, reflective and autonomous morality where moral values and standards are adhered to as a result of rational examination and reflection by the individual. Such a morality is a personal, individualised morality belonging to the person and which has not simply been taken from other people or societal institutions without personal reflection.

Developmental theory suggests that young children's moral understanding is initially at a primitive level. Special strategies and experience can assist young children to move towards the intermediate level which develops fully during the primary school and early secondary school years. The capacity for a mature morality develops during late adolescence and adulthood.

THEORETICAL EXPLANATIONS OF MORAL DEVELOPMENT

A number of theoretical perspectives propose different accounts of how morality develops in children and adults. Three different but equally valid theoretical explanations related to moral development are summarised below.

Psychoanalytic theory

One of the earliest explanations concerning how morality develops in children came from Freud's psychoanalytic theory which emphasises the importance of the development of a personality construct called the Superego and the associated constructs of the conscience and guilt.

Briefly, psychoanalytic theory proposes that children's beliefs about what is right and wrong (that is, moral beliefs) are based on the values and ideas of the particular culture in which the child is reared. The child adopts such values and beliefs through the process of identification with the same sexed parent and through adult use of rewards and punishment. Freud's theory of personality and the role of the Oedipal complex provides an explanation of the development and function of the conscience and guilt.

Put very simply, psychoanalytic theory argues that, around five years of age, the child develops a conscience which contains all the knowledge of the acts that deserve to be punished. The ego ideal contains all the information about acts that should be rewarded. When a child internalises this information, the conscience generates guilt which makes her feel uncomfortable when she does things considered to be bad or 'naughty'. On the other hand, when children engage in behaviours considered to be right or good, the ego ideal generates feelings of satisfaction and happiness. Such feelings motivate the child to engage in acceptable behaviour and to refrain from displaying unacceptable behaviour.

Human behaviour illustrates the limitations of this explanation. Conscience is not a reliable guide to behaviour. Many children and adults engage in behaviour they believe to be wrong, even though they feel guilty. In many cases, we are willing to tolerate intense guilt feelings in order to do what we want to do! We all develop different levels of guilt—some feel more guilt than others. Guilt is perceived as having the capacity to manipulate behaviour. Adults often use guilt to manipulate children's behaviour. This is rarely productive and usually results in children feeling anxious and apprehensive about the nature of their relationship with the adult. Given that all learning is dependent on trusting relationships between adults and children, the use of guilt is not considered to be a constructive approach to helping children learn to behave appropriately or as a strategy for nurturing moral development.

Learning theory

Current thinking about morality outlined in Berk (1991) and Eisenberg (1992) acknowledges that some moral behaviour, especially prosocial behaviour, has some biological roots. However, many other researchers argue that morality has its roots in the social world of human beings with each culture and society socialising or actively teaching a system of morality to its children. Learning theory explains this perspective. Socialisation is conducted by various agents in the society, such as, parents, officers of the church, religious teachers, teachers and other adults in care and educational systems, peers and the media. Morality is considered by theorists to be learned directly from the group in which one lives, through reward and punishment of certain behaviours, observation and modelling.

The impact of parents in the moral development of young children has recently been considered to be diminishing because of the proportion of time many children are spending with non-familial adults, such as caregivers, educators and teachers. Research by Bandura (1977) indicates that strong, enduring, difficult to change attitudes and values are formed by children by the age of five years. The development of moral behaviour and understanding is becoming increasingly important as non-familial adults, such as early childhood professionals take over the early socialisation of young children.

Many writers have referred to the impact that various parenting styles have on young children's moral development. Persuasive and authoritarian approaches to child rearing are considered to inhibit young children's moral development, whereas the authoritative and democratic approaches tend to be associated with the development of greater self control in young children. These latter approaches are characterised by adults who are affectionate and rewarding, reluctant to use physical punishment and who use rule-inductive rather than power-assertive discipline practices.

Cognitive-developmental theory

Although learning theory explains how morality is acquired from the social environment, just as any other behaviours, it appears that what is being explained is the process of social conformity where children learn to behave according to social convention without questioning the ethical basis of the behaviour. History has shown us that immoral acts have been engaged in by people who simply conformed to social norms without considering, or by disregarding, important ethical principles and goals. Young children have the capacity to learn to distinguish between social convention and issues of morality. However, they need opportunities, not to blindly follow and conform, but actively to think about their experiences in the social environment. Children appear to interact with the world in order to make sense out of rules and conventions. They begin to make moral judgements at a very young age, which indicates that reason begins to play a role in the development of morality. Once children start to think about the reasons behind behaviour, they begin to understand the social and interpersonal world in a more sophisticated way and have taken the first step in moving from a primitive understanding of morality to the intermediate level.

The cognitive-developmental approach to understanding young children's development was first proposed by Piaget in 1932. Although he agreed with the other theoretical viewpoints of his time which considered that young children's morality was largely a result of uncritical acceptance of adult prescriptions, he argued that morality was not a result of the internalisation of group norms or the adult acting upon the child. Piaget argued that children had a qualitatively different understanding of the social world compared to adult understanding. This pre-moral and primitive understanding underwent revision and changed as the child interacted with the social environment. Piaget was the first of a number of important cognitive-developmental theorists, such as Kohlberg, Hoffman, Selman, Damon and Eisenberg, who proposed that moral development and understanding changed with age. These theorists proposed a number of 'stage' theories in which children's reasoning capacities were described and characterised as revealing certain stages of development.

Piaget conceptualised children's morality as a series of stages in which moral concepts evolved in an unvarying sequence from pre-moral, motor ritualism (which involves habits and learned responses) to moral realism (heteronomous morality) and finally to moral relationism (autonomous morality). Children under two years of age were considered not to be capable of any moral understanding which developed gradually between approximately two and five years. Preschoolers' morality was considered to be characterised by the features of moral realism. Piaget argued that a long period of transition exists between five and approximately nine years when children gradually and inconsistently begin to show the characteristics of moral relationism in their thinking. This type of thinking becomes stable about twelve or thirteen years of age with more refined reasoning and judgements developing through adolescence and adulthood.

For Piaget, mature morality includes both the child's understanding and acceptance of social rules as well as the child's concern for equality and reciprocity in human relations as a basis for justice. The following points summarise the important characteristics of the two major stages described by Piaget:

Stage 1 Moral realism

- Rules are rules and not to be broken; rules are established by adult authority and taken for granted.
- The consequences of an act are seen as more important than the intentions of the person committing the act.
- Punishments are severe and designed to make the person feel as if she has 'paid' for misbehaviour.

- Immanent justice (the sense that misdeeds carry within them the seeds of their own punishment) is quite strong.

Stage 2 Moral relativism

- A more flexible approach to rules can be seen here. Rules can be changed to take account of different things. Rules are made by everybody and not just adults.
- Intentions can rationalise a misdeed. Accidental misdeeds are not as bad as those which are purposeful, and punishments are often altered in terms of intentionality of an act.
- Punishments are less likely to be harsh and seem to be more designed to 'make up' for the bad behaviour.
- Immanent justice is less strong. Children may still feel guilty, and that guilt may be related to the punishment, but they will probably be unable to verbalise this relationship.

Therefore, the child moves from a rigid, inflexible concept of justice dominated by adult authority, where right is right and wrong is wrong, to a concept of justice that involves flexibility and reciprocity.

Lawrence Kohlberg was one of Piaget's students and, after studying Piaget's stages of cognitive and moral development, he proposed his own theory of moral development which was derived from and extended Piaget's theory. Kohlberg thought that people progress through a stage sequence in the development of moral reasoning and understanding. He conceptualised moral development as having three levels:

- *Pre-conventional*, where there is no internalisation of moral standards,
- *Conventional*, where conformity to parents and peers rather than ethical standards defines morality, and
- *Post-conventional*, in which an internalised code of self accepted principles regulates moral judgements.

Within each level, he described two stages. So, Kohlberg's theory outlines three levels which incorporate a total of six stages. Progress from an earlier level and stage to a later level and stage was considered to be dependent upon experience, social interaction, feedback from others and increased ability in reasoning.

Kohlberg considered that children under approximately four years are pre-moral, not having yet developed the cognitive skills essential for moral understanding. For these children, right is what feels good and wrong is what feels painful or creates fear. Preschoolers (four to five years) function in Stage 1 of the pre-conventional level (right is what authority says is right) with some children aged six to seven years developing the abilities to function in Stage 2 of the pre-conventional level (right is what brings one some reward). Primary school children usually demonstrate Stage 3 thinking in the conventional level (peers establish what is right), with most people in society operating in Stage 4 thinking of the conventional level (law and order establish what is right).

An important point to note in both Piaget's and Kohlberg's theories is that people may have developed the ability to understand, think and reason at a certain level and stage but that, in day to day incidents, may function at lower and even the lowest levels and stages of moral understanding and reasoning. Possessing the capacity to think at a higher level or stage does not necessarily ensure that the ability will be applied to specific incidents.

While Piaget and Kohlberg have provided much insight into the development of moral understanding and reasoning, their value has been lessened for early childhood professionals and parents because although they have described the ways in which children understand the world they have not specifically outlined how to facilitate movement to and the acquisition of prerequisite skills for higher stage thinking.

Kuhmerker (1976) drew together the work of three other important cognitive-developmental theorists whose work has complemented that of Piaget and Kohlberg. These theorists, Hoffman, Selman and Damon, argued that moral development depended upon the ability to de-centre as well as the acquisition of specific cognitive skills. Each stage of moral development was considered to depend on the attainment of certain levels of cognitive skills in order to enable the cognitive re-organisation that is necessary to move to a higher stage. They considered that the three most important cognitive skills for young children to acquire were empathy, perspective or role taking skills and concepts of distributive justice as a basis for understanding fairness.

Hoffman constructed a stage theory for the development of empathy in children. Basically, he argues that children proceed through the following four stages:

1 Sympathetic distress reaction

This is the stage in which babies up to about fifteen months are capable of responding to another's distress. However, the infant does not possess the cognitive capacity to comprehend which particular person is in distress. Examples of this stage are neonate babies crying when they hear other babies crying in the nursery. Alternatively, a toddler may see another child fall and look as if she will cry as well, or indeed, begin to cry too.

2 Person permanence

This is the stage in which a child (fifteen months to three years) understands distress cues and now knows who is experiencing distress. However, the child may be unaware that the distressed person may have different needs or point of view from her own. Consequently, the child's response to the distressed child may be inappropriate. Examples of behaviour in this stage are children bringing bandaids to children who may be upset at separation, bringing their own mother to comfort a crying child, offering their own comforter to an upset peer and asking 'What's the matter, what's wrong?'

3 Role taking

In this stage, from approximately three to seven years, young children are able to take the perspective of another person, imagine themselves in that position and therefore respond appropriately to the child's needs. Children need to have the skills of Level 1 in Selman's theory (Kuhmerker, 1976), which is outlined in the following section, to move to this stage of development in empathy. Examples of behaviour in this stage are children comforting a friend who has lost a prized possession, money or done poorly on a test. Sharing a sandwich with someone who forgot to bring their lunch is another example.

4 Comprehensive empathy

This is a capacity in older children (eight upwards) to understand distress and emotions within the broader context—that is people from completely different situations to their own, such as people starving in war torn countries, sick children in hospital, the less fortunate. The capacity for empathy in chronic as well as acute situations develops. Examples of behaviour at this stage are collecting for charity, participating in the Walk Against Want or the 40 Hour Famine, or helping elderly people with their garden.

In the development of morality, it is essential to understand the importance of being able to take another person's point of view or perspective. The following points summarise Selman's first three levels and the characteristics of each level. Levels 0, 1 and 2 are relevant for early childhood professionals who can offer experiences to assist young children in developing their perspective taking and role taking skills.

Level 0 Egocentric perspective taking (Two to four years)

Although the child can identify superficial emotions in other people, she often confuses other's perspectives with her own. She does not realise that others may see a social situation differently from the way she does.

Level 1 Subjective perspective taking (Three to five years)

Child begins to understand that other people's thoughts and feelings may be the same or different from hers. She realises that people feel differently or think differently because they are in different situations or have different information.

Level 2 Self-reflective perspective taking (Four to seven years)

The child is able to reflect on her own thoughts and feelings. She can anticipate other's perspective on her own thoughts and feelings and realise that this influences her perspective on others.

Finally, young children's understanding of distributive justice has been shown to be related to the capacity for and level of moral reasoning. Damon's (1977) work is important here. Damon showed that young children's understanding of justice or fairness developed in six age-related stages. Stengel (1982: 24–25) summarised Damon's stages in a framework which is useful for understanding young children's attitudes about justice and fairness. It is easier to understand Damon's stages if you consider the example of asking a young child to justify her choices about how a bag of sweets should be shared between a group of children.

Level 0 A (Four years)

Fairness is equated with the child's egocentric desires and wishes, for example, 'I should get all the sweets because I want them'. The reasons simply assert the choices with no attempt to justify a particular choice.

Level 0 B (Four to five years)

Fairness is equated with the child's egocentric needs or illogical external characteristics, such as size, gender or other physical characteristics, for example, 'I should get four sweets because I'm four' or 'I should get the most because I'm the tallest'. These justifications are inconsistent and ultimately self serving, with fairness being confused with niceness.

Level 1 A (Five years)

Fairness is equated with strict equality. Everyone should get the same and no special consideration should be given to anyone, for example, 'We all should get exactly the same amount of sweets'. Justifications are consistent with the principle of equality but are unilateral and inflexible.

Level 1 B (Six to seven years)

Fairness is equated with merit and reciprocity. Those who work harder or put in more effort should get more, for example, 'I put away the most blocks and worked the hardest so I should get more sweets than anyone else'. Justifications are based on the notion that people should be paid back in kind for the good and bad things they do. Fairness is confused with deserving and merit.

Level 2 A (Eight years)

Fairness is influenced by different but equally valid claims and special consideration is given for special needs, for example, 'She should get some sweets because she's only little and shouldn't have to work as hard as the older children'. Justifications are based on compromises between competing claims. Fairness is confused with compromise.

Level 2 B (Eight years plus)

Fairness is relative with the claims of the various people involved and the demands of the specific situation considered in its determination. Everyone should be given a fair share. Justifications are firm and clear cut and reflect the recognition that all persons should be given their due and this may not result in equal treatment. Fairness is considered to relate to the satisfaction of all persons involved.

Early childhood professionals can stimulate young children's development of understanding of justice and fairness by providing them with meaningful opportunities to share and distribute resources such as food, toys and time with equipment, while at the same time discussing with them the reasons behind their choices. This helps young children to take the perspective of others and to learn that reasons are important in stating their own viewpoint.

MORAL DEVELOPMENT AND PROSOCIAL BEHAVIOUR

Moral behaviour comprises many aspects. Among these is a prosocial orientation which is taken to mean helping, comforting, sharing or rescuing behaviour on the part of one person to another person. For prosocial behaviour to be termed 'altruistic', the actions engaged in must be intended to help or benefit another person or group without any anticipation or expectation of external reward.

The majority of writing and research on understanding moral development has been focused on understanding the factors that contribute to negative behaviour: the anti-social, unacceptable or prohibited behaviour. This is sometimes referred to as a 'prohibitive morality'. On the other hand, there has been increasing interest by researchers into the positive aspects of social interaction and the factors that contribute to helping, sharing and comforting. The major researcher in this area is Nancy Eisenberg who reports her own research, and that of others, into the obvious interest in and capacity even very young children possess for prosocial (as distinct from altruistic) behaviour.

Although prosocial behaviour is valued in many societies as a characteristic of mature human beings who can, and choose, to act in a socially responsible manner (such as showing concern for our companions, helping and nurturing others when it is in our power to do so), numerous developmental theorists, including Freud and Piaget, claimed that young children were oriented to and interested only in themselves. Young children were considered to be egocentric, interested only in having their own needs met rather than in meeting the needs of others. Such theorists argued that genuine concern for others was developed in older children and adolescents. Yet, parents and early childhood professionals have reported observation of prosocial behaviour in children as young as 12 months of age as well as a gradual but increasing frequency of such behaviour as children grow older (Eisenberg, 1992). It must be noted that despite this developmental trend, great individual variation exists in relation to whether young children will respond prosocially to another child. While many children have the capacity to do so, they may not always behave prosocially due to a range of factors, including important contextual determinants.

While many developmental theorists argue that young children's cognitive and affective skills may not be fully developed, the fact that young children spontaneously engage in prosocial behaviours suggests that there must be sufficient development in skills which enable a certain responsiveness. These skills appear to steadily improve and develop with age, experience and opportunities actively to practice them which produce a more sophisticated, appropriate and complex responsiveness. However, it appears that poor development in such skills, for example, empathy, perspective taking, moral reasoning, precludes prosocial responsiveness.

Eisenberg (1992) has approached moral development from a different perspective. Instead of examining moral and ethical prohibitions, she investigated 'prescriptive morality', that is, the prescriptions or rules about how one should behave positively in relation to others. She developed her own cognitive-developmental theory of prosocial reasoning which was based on children's responses to dilemmas similar to those used by Kohlberg.

To conclude this discussion on prosocial development, it is evident that young children are, at least to some degree, capable of understanding others' feelings and of engaging in empathic, prosocial actions. Their understanding of, and reasoning about, prosocial incidents is qualitatively different to that of adults and changes over time from a more primitive understanding to a more sophisticated grasp of the complexity of the situation. Not all children (and adults) are equally prosocial in disposition. However, it is evident that certain cognitive skills, socialisation experiences and specific situations which offer opportunities for prosocial responding are necessary to nurture prosocial responsiveness.

STIMULATING YOUNG CHILDREN'S MORAL UNDERSTANDING AND BEHAVIOUR

An understanding of moral development and education has a number of outcomes for the early childhood professional. First, it develops understanding about an important aspect of human development and interaction. Second, it focuses attention on techniques and activities which foster the development of moral understanding and behaviour in young children. Third, early childhood professionals who have thought through their own ideas about morality are in a good position to help guide children through the ethical situations encountered in day to day living and interaction with other people. In addition, early childhood professionals can help children develop self direction, self control, self discipline, responsibility and cooperative orientation, all of which need to be mastered by people to become fully functioning members of society.

There is a close link between moral development and the strategies adults use to respond to children's behaviour. The question 'who raises a morally mature child?' is important for parents and early childhood professionals alike. The development of self control is a central feature of morally mature individuals.

Since young children tend to be egocentric and self centred, they need many opportunities to become involved in the feelings, needs and situation (or perspective) of others. Involving children in role playing where they assume the character's role and try out behaviours and attitudes is helpful. Providing opportunities for children to view and understand a situation from another's point of view or perspective is also valuable. The research literature (Buzzelli, 1992) has shown that training and practice are important here.

Empathy has been shown to be an essential basis for the development of prosocial and moral responsiveness. Following are some ways of developing young children's capacity for empathy:

1   Quietly sitting with a child to discuss with her the effects on the family or group of some inappropriate action of hers.
2   Helping a child work through a decision by provoking consideration of the feelings of others who will be affected by the decision—for example, whether to cancel an earlier commitment to play with a friend when a more interesting invitation is issued from another friend.
3   Adults sharing with children their feelings about encounters or events that affect them.
4   Helping children clarify their feelings about encounters or events that affect them.
5   Acknowledging and discussing with the children those times when their actions or presence were a source of joy, pleasure, courage or comfort.

Basically, early childhood professionals want to help children develop a sense of community in the family, the early childhood centre and in all of the groups to which they belong. Later this understanding of community will expand to include the larger community of humankind, but the quality of concern at that time is dependent on the earlier sensitivity to smaller communities.

Empathy and mutual respect should be the focus of moral education programs for young children, since it is the ability to understand from another's perspective that enables them to participate more fully in the family, child care centres, preschools and peer communities. It is this function, the developing of empathy by stimulating the child to put herself in another's position, that Kohlberg found to be the most important contribution of the family, caregivers and teachers in moral development.

PRACTICAL STRATEGIES FOR EARLY CHILDHOOD PROFESSIONALS

The following suggestions can assist early childhood professionals to enhance the development of young children's moral understanding and behaviour.

1   Focus on establishing the group as a community where the children will live and learn together in an atmosphere of respect and security.
2   Provide opportunities for the children to have a voice in establishing the rules of the group.

3 Choose consequences that relate to the offence, stressing with the child, where possible, the effect of her action on the group.
4 Make distinctions between criticism of young children's learning efforts and criticism of their behaviour, and between rules for the good order of the early childhood centre or group and rules affecting justice and human relations.
5 Provide opportunities for peer group work.
6 In stories and discussions of everyday experience, help the children to consider the feelings of other real or fictional persons.
7 Role play experiences from daily life, such as events that lead to disappointments, tensions, fights, joys in order to provide opportunities for the children to see the event from perspectives other than their own.
8 Discuss with the group what they consider to be fair and unfair rules, procedures and relationships.
9 Frequently take time to listen to each child's responses to questions of moral judgement and stimulate discussions that will provoke higher stage reasoning, using literature, film and life experiences.
10 Avoid making judgements about moral development on the basis of behaviour.

Early childhood professionals can help parents enhance the moral behaviour, understanding and reasoning of their children by suggesting relevant, age-appropriate ways of interacting with and responding to moral incidents, such as:

1 Refraining from equating rule observance and obedience with moral development.
2 Attending to and actively asking for children's reasons for their moral judgements.
3 Refraining from evaluating reasons as good or bad or decisions as right or wrong.
4 Making distinctions in concern between rules for good manners and good household order and issues of moral substance concerning justice and human relations.
5 Providing opportunities for children to participate in deciding rules for common living in the family.
6 Avoiding attempts to stimulate the child's moral reasoning when in the heat of anger and aggravation over behaviour.

7   Selecting consequences that relate to the specific offences and that emphasise the effect of behaviour on the family or community.
8   Trying not to react with more anger or disgust to children's carelessness than to the same action committed by an adult.
9   Tempering reactions to the young child's distasteful epithets and imaginative fibs.
10 Respecting the child's right to an apology when you have been unjust in condemnation or judgement.
11 Being patient with children's delicate sense of justice when they refuse to perform even an inconsequential act like closing the door because they judge the command unfair, that is, because they were not the last one in! If possible, avoid resorting to an authoritarian role by conveying to them the understanding that you are asking them for a favour. But note, they still may refuse!
12 Periodically discussing with the children what they consider to be fair and unfair in the family relationships and procedures.
13 Encouraging children to assume responsibility for establishing procedures for dividing up the household chores and responsibilities.
14 Discussing contemporary issues that involve moral decisions and urging each child to articulate her position and reasons, but being careful not to evaluate any responses or decisions as right or wrong, or as better or best.
15 Focusing on reasons for judgement, not on the child's behaviour.
16 Being realistic in your expectations, remembering that it is approximately twenty years before the young adult judges from the perspective of the general social order.
17 Setting up structures for living and articulating expectations for conduct, but remembering that parents cannot imprint their own values on their children. In order to construct their own system of values, children have to rethink and order those which adults projected.

Although early childhood professionals sometimes feel frustrated when young children appear blatantly to break the rules and social conventions, responses such as laying down the law, punishing children in some way, ignoring children, explaining yet again about why the rule exists, do not appear to encourage young children to act in more morally mature ways (Houghton and McColgan, 1995). It is important to remember that power assertiveness does not nurture moral development but may produce a child who will only comply and follow rules when someone in authority is present. Such children can be excessively influenced by a domineering person (adult or peer) with whom they associate. Love withdrawal techniques often result in anxiety, apprehension about the relationship and feelings of worthlessness which have a negative impact on secure relationships between adults and children. To obtain the highest level of morality in children, discipline based on rule induction, that is, the use of explanation and reasoning appears to be most effective.

5

WHAT DO ADULTS WANT FROM YOUNG CHILDREN?

Expectations and goals about young children's behaviour

Discipline and behaviour management are based on personal values and experience as well as professional values and experience, therefore contain an element which is highly subjective. While most adults, early childhood professionals and parents included, have strong ideas about how young children's behaviour should be managed, these are often highly personal, emotional and based upon their own experience. The old adage 'I was punished as a child and it didn't hurt me' still can be heard in some early childhood centres! The limitation of this approach is that it recognises that young children do need to be taught social and cultural expectations and to behave in appropriate ways. However, rarely do adults ask 'What do I want to achieve in children's behaviour?', 'What is the purpose of behaviour management?' or 'What are my goals in working to help children become self disciplined?'.

Because approaches to behaviour management have an enormous effect on young children's learning, self concept and self esteem, it is critical that early childhood professionals select and implement approaches which are conducive to young children's growth, development and learning. To do this, early childhood professionals need to identify their goals, that is, what they want to achieve in their work with young children. As well as setting goals for development and learning in the physical, intellectual, language, social, emotional and moral areas, early childhood

70

professionals have a responsibility to understand their goals in behaviour management and to include these in their program planning and curriculum development.

It is recognised that early childhood professionals receive very little guidance in their curriculum decisions (Schiller and Cohen, 1988) and even fewer guidelines are available when it comes to decisions about how to respond to children's need for behavioural guidance. Rogers (1989) suggested that, in determining how and when to respond to children's inappropriate behaviour, adults could use the following three criteria: the protection of children's safety, the assurance of fair treatment, and mutual respect. Grossman's (1995) categories of non problem behaviour, minor problem behaviour and major problem behaviour also may provide the early childhood professional with guidelines for defining a hierarchy of problematic behaviour and for considering the types of management strategies which may be relevant and effective for the different categories of behaviours. Gartrell's (1995) differentiation between mistaken behaviour, as opposed to misbehaviour, is also a useful framework for understanding and deciding how to respond to young children's behaviour. He suggested that mistaken behaviour could be categorised into three levels. In Level 3, mistaken behaviour, such as withdrawal and acting out, is thought to be a result of strong psychological needs. Mistaken behaviour at Level 3 may be symptomatic of other problems arising from factors such as stress or emotional pain. In Level 2, mistaken behaviour is considered to be a result of the social influence, for example by peers or the media. Level 1 describes mistaken behaviour which is a result of young children's experimentation and quest for autonomy.

In general, the guidelines suggested by government regulatory bodies, such as the State of Victoria's Office of Preschool and Child Care (1992), which are provided for early childhood professionals in relation to curriculum decisions propose that these decisions should be based upon:

• Knowledge and understanding of child development and processes of learning which give indications about young children's level of development, what they are capable of learning and how best to teach them.

• Awareness of cultural and social values and assumptions which should be used to guide decisions about what is to be taught as well as how to teach it.

In addition, early childhood professionals have been provided with documentation in relation to general standards of practice and codes of ethics, such as have been developed by the National Association for the Education of Young Children (NAEYC) in America and the Australian Early Childhood Association (1991). In an attempt to be more specific about acceptable, professional practice, NAEYC (1984) and the National Childcare Accreditation Council of Australia (1993) have outlined specific principles which are related to quality approaches to behaviour management in their documents for voluntary accreditation. For example, in Australia's Quality Improvement and Accreditation System, Principle 4 states 'Staff use a positive approach in guidance and discipline' and Principle 7 states 'Staff show respect for children's developing competence and foster their self esteem and independence'. While some examples of High Quality, Good Quality, Basic Quality and Unsatisfactory responses are provided for each principle, no further details are provided for staff to help them implement the principles appropriately. Consequently, despite these resources and guidelines, early childhood professionals have enormous latitude and freedom to choose how to respond to and manage young children's behaviour. Professional and responsible early childhood personnel will seek to act in ways which are consistent with professional values. However, there are still few consequences for those early childhood professionals who continue to choose to engage in practices which are regarded by the field to be detrimental to young children's well being. One way of assisting early childhood professionals to adopt behaviour management strategies which are favourable for young children's development is for them to understand that behaviour management is part of the overall program or curriculum, that it contains goals and that there are relevant and effective strategies available which facilitate the achievement of their goals.

CURRICULUM AND BEHAVIOUR MANAGEMENT

A curriculum has two elements. First, it includes the process of deciding what to teach, how to teach, when to teach and how to evaluate the intended and unintended outcomes of teaching and any modifications to the process of teaching as a result of these decisions. Second, it is a product in that it is a written document which sets out the planned learning experiences for children based on clear professional values and goals, the strategies for implementing the learning experiences and the processes for evaluating the impact of these learning experiences on children. It is important that early childhood professionals are clear about what a program or curriculum involves and how approaches to behaviour management fit into it.

A professional approach to behaviour management in early childhood centres needs to contain all of the above elements of a curriculum. Early childhood professionals should be able to communicate to other staff and parents the following information:

1   What they want to teach children in behaviour management incidents.
2   How they will teach what they want the children to learn from behaviour management incidents.
3   Understanding about the importance of timeliness in the use of behaviour management techniques, including awareness about the importance of the 'teachable moment'.
4   How they will evaluate the success or otherwise of their selected behaviour management strategies.
5   How they will identify intended and any unintended outcomes of their approach to behaviour management.
6   How they will refine or modify their approach to behaviour management for future incidents based upon the above information.

In addition, early childhood professionals will have included in their overall written program or curriculum planning document, individual and group goals for children's learning experiences in relation to developing self control and self discipline, specific strategies for achieving these goals and the means for evaluating the impact of behavioural learning experiences on children.

Given current community and parental interest in quality for early childhood programs, it is essential that early childhood professionals understand parental and community concern with behaviour management practices. Accountability is a catch cry in today's society and early childhood professionals are required to be accountable in relation to the social and ethical values that underpin their curricula and practices to children, parents, managing committees, auspicing bodies and government departments. In relation to behaviour management, one way of early childhood professionals ensuring that they are accountable is for them to develop and write down the philosophy behind the goals and practices implemented for behaviour management in the curriculum.

When beginning to reflect upon the basis of behaviour management in the early childhood curriculum, early childhood professionals need to consider parental, community and societal values and assumptions, professional and government expectations and requirements and the latest research about quality and effective early care and educational practices. In addition, a professional approach to behaviour management in the curriculum includes knowledge of and information about young children's developmental needs, staff values and preferences, staff knowledge, skills and experience and the centre's philosophy and culture. All of this information is useful when setting the goals of behaviour management.

THE GOALS OF BEHAVIOUR MANAGEMENT

For early childhood professionals, a goal is a simple statement of intended outcomes based on value judgements about what is considered important for young children to learn. Early childhood professionals need to reflect upon what it is that they want to achieve in behaviour management. This requires a broad perspective because the overall goal in early childhood professionals' work with young children is to foster their developmental potential so that they can become fully functioning, competent and responsible adults in their culture and society. While it is certainly helpful to nurture characteristics and behaviours that make young children easier to manage, this may not serve the overall goal which is to produce adults who can function in society (Fields and Boesser, 1994). This means that the first step in defining the goals of behaviour management is to ask 'What sort of adult do I want this child to grow up to be?'. It is likely that the answer to this question will include characteristics which tend to be associated with adult-like characteristics and behaviours.

In addition to early childhood professionals reflecting upon the issue of what type of adults are valued in their culture and society, they also need to understand the sources of inappropriate behaviour in young children. Three major sources of inappropriate behaviour are: first, inappropriate behaviour which has been learned intentionally or unintentionally by young children from parents, siblings, peers and media; second, poor self concept and low self esteem; and third, social problems, such as inappropriate notions of how to belong, lack of interest in meeting the needs of others and discouragement. The information gleaned from these three areas points to three different types of goals for managing young children's behaviour: short term, long term and educational.

SHORT TERM GOALS

Early childhood professionals have many responsibilities when it comes to their work with young children. They are responsible for their safety and well being, for nurturing their development and also for teaching them knowledge and skills which are considered by their culture to be appropriate for their age and stage of development. They are responsible for fostering development and learning both in individual children and with a small or large group of children. Much of this work requires a long time span. However, if individual children or a group of children interact in a way which prevents the early childhood professional from fulfilling certain aspects of her role and responsibilities, it is important that measures be taken in the short term in order to create and maintain an environment which is conducive to optimum learning by young children. Therefore, a short term goal of behaviour management for early childhood professionals is to manage young children's behaviour in ways that will reduce or eliminate inappropriate behaviour and at the same time encourage and increase socially and culturally acceptable, mature and competent behaviour.

When defining short term goals, it is essential that early childhood professionals specify in clear and concrete terms what it is they want to achieve within a predefined time span. For example, some early childhood professionals have defined a short term goal as 'children being less aggressive and more cooperative'. This is too broad because it is not clear which particular behaviours are referred to. It will also take a considerable period of time for some young children to be able to gain control over this behaviour and replace it with a more acceptable one. Aggression includes biting, kicking, pinching, spitting, hitting, punching, pulling, swearing, destroying and so on. Cooperation could include following instructions, packing away, cleaning up, being empathic to the needs of others, expressing feelings with appropriate language, helping, comforting, rescuing, protecting and so on. Short term goals are essential for responding to any dangerous or destructive behaviour.

Young children learn better if early childhood professionals work with only one or two behaviours at a time. Therefore, it is essential that the behaviours which early childhood professionals wish to decrease and increase are defined in clear, specific and concrete terms. For example, 'For Val to stop punching Marcus', 'For Sally to hang her smock up on the peg after painting' and 'For Jamal to stop using four letter words and express feelings of anger with acceptable language such as "sugar" or "fiddlesticks"'.

In order to create an atmosphere in which young children can learn, some behaviours need to be attended to by early childhood professionals immediately and decreased or increased in the short term. The selection of behaviour management techniques to achieve these goals needs to be consistent with the development of young children's self concept and self esteem (see Chapters 3 and 7) and independence (see Chapters 8 and 9). However, early childhood professionals are cautioned not to equate a quiet group which is controlled by authoritarian methods with an optimum learning environment. The detrimental effects of a punitive environment on young children's learning are discussed in Chapter 7.

LONG TERM GOALS

Most early childhood professionals are aware that it takes young children many years and considerable experience to learn to control their own behaviour in accordance with social and cultural expectations and standards. This can be a frustrating aspect of the early childhood professional's work because the outcome of the work and effort that they put in with young children is rarely experienced. Often, it is primary and secondary teachers who are the beneficiaries of the time, thought and effort that early childhood professionals take to lay the foundation for a self disciplined and self controlled child.

Long term goals for behaviour management provide early childhood professionals with direction and purpose for responding to behavioural incidents. This is important because a tendency to use short term, quick fix methods in an ad hoc manner will not help young children in the long term learn how to behave in mature and acceptable ways. Early childhood professionals may end up treating the symptom and not the cause of behaviour difficulties if they do not focus more broadly. The problem is not eliminated, it merely presents itself in another form. It is the long term goals which reflect the early childhood professional's analysis of what young children need to learn and how best to teach them that provide the basis of behaviour management within a curriculum or program and determine the day to day decision making processes in relation to behaviour management.

Two important long term goals of behaviour management are:

- For young children to learn effective communication skills which contribute to the development of positive interpersonal relationships.
- For young children to develop self discipline, responsibility and cooperation.

While most early childhood professionals accept these as legitimate goals, there can be disagreement about how to achieve them. Behaviourists base their approach on the work of Watson, Skinner and Bandura (Marion, 1991) and take a more authoritarian perspective (Rodd and Holland, 1990) which is known as 'behaviour modification' and more recently as 'applied behaviour analysis'. They believe that reward and punishment shape behaviour and aim to obtain obedience from children. Maturationists, on the other hand, accept Gessell's ideas about how children develop and consequently tend to be more permissive, believing that development over time gives young children the maturity necessary to learn what is required from them. Humanists, such as Carl Rogers (who coined the term 'active listening'), Glasser and Gordon focus upon the individual freedom of children. Cognitive-developmentalists base their approach on Piaget's ideas and want children to become self disciplined and responsible (Fields and Boesser, 1994). Finally, Adlerians, such as Dreikurs and Dinkmeyer and McKay want to foster social interest in young children and help them find appropriate ways or goals of behaviour for belonging in a group. It is important to remember that behaviour management for young children is about guidance and helping children learn rather than coercion and instruction.

(Gordon, 1991). Therefore, the methods selected to achieve the long term goals should be consistent with the developmental view which argues that young children learn more effectively when they are able to make decisions and choices, to solve their problems independently and are acknowledged for their efforts to meet the needs of the situation. Techniques related to the developmental view that children learn from their experience are discussed in Chapters 9 and 10.

EDUCATIONAL GOALS

Early childhood professionals have a major responsibility to deliver educational curricula and programs to individuals and groups of young children in ways that assist young children both to learn and become socialised. Young children do not come into the world with prior knowledge about social and cultural expectations and standards, they have to learn them. The responsible early childhood professionals will understand that part of their work with young children is to educate, teach and help them learn about social conventions, that is, what is acceptable and unacceptable behaviour. When early childhood professionals set educational goals for young children, they are in fact engaging a preventive approach to discipline which is discussed in Chapter 6. In addition, while they are teaching and children are learning, early childhood professionals are offering a supportive approach to behaviour management by their use of positive management techniques. If a corrective approach is necessary, positive redirection of behaviour, direct teaching and explanation might be useful strategies.

Some examples of educational goals for young children in relation to behaviour management are:

'We take care of our and others' property.'
'We do not hurt, damage and destroy other living things.'
'We help each other to get things done.'
'We share out the cake fairly.'
'We tell the truth.'

Educational goals related to behaviour management need to be realistic with expectations and standards set neither too high or too low. They need to enable young children to gain satisfaction and confidence from mastering the challenges set by their culture and society so that young children do not need to engage in unacceptable behaviour to meet their own needs.

DEALING WITH CAUSES NOT SYMPTOMS

Sometimes early childhood professionals discover that, despite all their thought and efforts to respond constructively to a management situation, the situation continues or becomes worse. Under these circumstances, further analysis of the situation is required in order to ascertain the cause of the behaviour. There are a number of different reasons why inappropriate behaviour continues in young children despite the efforts of well meaning early childhood professionals. Fields and Boesser (1994) have identified a number of underlying causes which early childhood professionals need to be aware of.

1   Continued so-called 'misbehaviour' may not be that at all. It may be developmentally appropriate but annoying and troublesome behaviour. Some examples of behaviour which is typical of young children's developmental limitations are tantrums, biting, physical aggression, inability to share, pants wetting and soiling as well as angry and explosive expressions of frustration. Rather than attempting to change the behaviour, a preventive approach to the problem would be more likely to be successful. Early childhood professionals who do not understand or are intolerant of young children's developmental needs will continue to experience such problems until they become better informed about or change their attitude to such behaviours.

2   Unreasonable and inappropriate expectations set by early childhood professionals will cause behaviour problems with young children because they require children to produce behaviour of which they may be incapable. Early childhood professionals need to have a thorough understanding of child development in order to set expectations at levels which match young children's capabilities. The Office of Preschool and Child Care, Victoria (1992) posed some questions that early childhood professionals can ask themselves in relation to their expectations. The following questions have been modified on the basis of that document:

- Do I use my knowledge of child development as the basis of my goals and planning?
- In what ways do my goals relate to young children's competence in physical, language, intellectual, social, emotional and moral development?
- Do my goals accommodate a range of developmental levels and allow for individual differences in children?
- Do my goals provide opportunities for children to develop their strengths, self concept, self esteem and skills?

In addition, the environment may be arranged in such a fashion which creates behavioural problems for young children. The importance of providing an environment which is conducive to learning and takes a preventive approach to behaviour management is discussed in Chapter 6.

3   Sometimes young children's inappropriate behaviour is a result of lack of knowledge about what is expected of them in a given situation. Living in a group care and educational setting is a new and challenging experience for many young children which requires knowledge and skills which they may not yet have acquired. Some children come from families who are very permissive and who have not taught their children community held expectations and standards. Other families have a life style which is vastly different from the mainstream in which children are taught quite different values and standards from the mainstream society.

When young children engage in certain behaviours, such as taking other people's possessions or not wearing underpants, lack of knowledge or different knowledge may be the cause. The early childhood professional's responsibility in such a case is to encourage the child to learn the general community held standards and expectations for group living. While parental values and wishes need to be respected and considered, it is not in a young child's best interests to be kept ignorant of community expectations regarding behaviour. The child will become a victim by experiencing consequences for choices that were not available to her. It is social reality that young children need to learn certain knowledge and skills in order to survive in society.

4   Some young children take longer than others to learn communication and social skills which enable them to function

capably in a group situation. In the same way as with knowledge, some children do not live in families where there are adequate opportunities to communicate and interact in socially acceptable ways. For example, some families solve interpersonal conflict with aggression and violence. Other families may believe that their impoverished circumstances make it acceptable for them to take whatever they need from whomever, and whenever they want to. Children who act in accordance with their family's values and norms are not misbehaving—they simply do not have the skills for behaving in any other way. It is the responsibility of the early childhood professional to help them to learn appropriate ways of communicating as well as interpersonal skills for social and group situations.

5   Experience is the best teacher for young children. However, some well intentioned early childhood professionals want to protect young children from experiencing the natural and logical consequences of their behaviour. It is essential to keep young children from harm. Nevertheless, early childhood professionals need to consider in every case whether the child would learn more from experiencing reasonable consequences than from an adult saying, 'I'll let you go swimming in your underpants this time. But next time you must have your swim suit.' Young children learn that the rules can be tested and broken from such a statement.

It can sometimes be difficult to distinguish behavioural consequences from punishment. Balson (1994) provides clear criteria for differentiating between these two strategies. With punishment, the adult assumes responsibility for the child's behaviour, decides what the child will do, asserts power over the child and offers no choice for the child. Punishment may be unrelated to the behaviour, is personalised, oriented to the past and is retaliatory. When adults apply a behavioural consequence, children take responsibility for their own behaviour, decide what to do and have choices about what to do. Behavioural consequences permit the reality of the natural or social order to take effect, are logically related to the behaviour, are impersonal, present or future oriented and are non-retaliatory.

6   Young children learn all sorts of behaviours from all sorts of areas including siblings, peers, media as well as from adults.

Adults, parents and early childhood professionals alike, are not able to control what young children learn or indeed teach them only appropriate behaviours. Lack of knowledge or experience in adults about how best to encourage children to learn appropriate behaviours, as well as the variety of learning opportunities to which young children are exposed, may result in young children learning behaviours which are regarded as unacceptable. It is important for early childhood professionals to consider whether the behaviour displayed is a case of inappropriate learning, that is the child has learned unwanted behaviours, for example, swearing. In such cases, ignoring the unwanted behaviour while at the same time teaching and rewarding more acceptable behaviour is a solution to the problem.

7   Some children display inappropriate behaviour because they have low self esteem, they do not feel that they have a place in or belong to the group, they are discouraged or they have unmet emotional needs of some sort. In an attempt to feel good about themselves, they may engage in a range of undesirable behaviours, such as being silly, aggressive, destructive or withdrawing. The long term solution to such behaviour is to identify the goals of misbehaviour which are discussed in Chapter 9. In addition, it may be necessary to use some short term strategies to minimise the inappropriate behaviour and provide opportunities to reward the appropriate behaviour that the child does engage in.

8   It is important for early childhood professionals to recognise that some young children have problems which require the skills of other professionals, such as medical doctors, audiologists, psychologists, counsellors and other therapists. If a child's behaviour is resistant to the efforts of an early childhood professional over some reasonable time period, it is important to advise parents to seek a referral to or consultation with an appropriate specialist. Every child has the right to the expertise of specialist knowledge and skills. Given that early childhood professionals have extensive knowledge about young children's general developmental norms and the kinds of behaviours that fall within and outside the norms, they are in a good position to judge whether the young child is in need of specialised assessment and intervention.

WHOSE PROBLEM IS IT?

An analysis of the causes of behaviour problems reveals that some of the problems are to do with the adult or are 'owned' by the early childhood professional. Early childhood professionals may need to respond to such causes by changing their expectations or the situation, removing themselves from the situation or communicating using an 'I' message. Where the cause appears to be associated with the child and the child 'owns' the problem, the early childhood professional may need to use active listening skills or natural and logical consequences.

Many early childhood professionals attempt to solve young children's problems for them rather than encouraging and supporting them to solve them themselves. Gordon (1970) termed this 'problem ownership'. Early childhood professionals need to be able to identify problems according to who owns them.

Early childhood professionals 'own the problem' when the child's behaviour is interfering with their rights (for example, when a child interrupts the early childhood professional's telephone call making it difficult to continue with the call) and that of the overall group (for example, when a child is making so much noise that a story cannot be read or when toys are left on the path so that someone may trip over them). In such cases, the early childhood professional needs to identify the problem as one she should deal with and take a problem solving approach by confronting the child with a statement, such as, 'I have a problem that I need your help with'. The communication skills discussed in Chapter 8 are helpful here.

Children own the problem when their behaviour indicates that their needs are not being met, for example, Anne does not like it when George calls her 'Carrots' because of her red hair or Spiros is frustrated because his collage has not finished up in a way that he wanted. Early childhood professionals can use their communication skills to teach the child that the problem is her own and to use problem solving skills by saying, 'You seem to have a problem. What do you need to do about it?'

Sometimes both children and adults own the problem because, if children's behaviour is interfering with the group's needs, then we all have a problem. In this case, the early childhood professional would initiate a mutual problem solving discussion by saying, 'Many children are not packing away the equipment at the end of outdoor play. This is a problem because we cannot begin anything new until all the equipment is in the shed. What are *we* going to do about it?' Similarly, when turn taking becomes an issue, the early childhood professional might say, 'We have a problem here. We cannot start riding the tricycle until we agree who is to have first turn. How can we sort this out?'

In conclusion, it is important for early childhood professionals to analyse, reflect upon and understand what it is that they expect from young children in relation to behaviour. It is unfortunate that while considerable time is allocated to other areas of the curriculum in planning, many early childhood professionals do not give the same amount of attention to planning for behaviour management. When early childhood professionals respond in ad hoc ways to behavioural incidents, they are not utilising their specialist knowledge and skills to produce the most effective outcome. Because behaviour management for young children is about helping children learn, teaching and guidance, this is an area which deserves and needs considerable thought and planning because it is part of the curriculum—it underpins and impinges upon the successful implementation of other areas of the curriculum or program. When early childhood professionals are clear about what it is they expect from young children and what their goals are, they will find that behaviour management is not the onerous task it once was. In fact, it can be an area where early childhood professionals can experience their greatest sense of achievement with young children.

6

PROBLEM PREVENTION

Making life easier for young children and adults

When living and working with young children, it is important for adults to understand that behaviour management is more about problem prevention than correction, more about helping children learn, teaching and guiding than demanding compliance and coercion (Gordon, 1991). Effective behaviour management is educative rather than punitive (Clewett, 1988).

Early childhood professionals are more likely to maintain positive attitudes to themselves and the children they work with if they take a preventive approach to discipline problems with young children. Many early childhood professionals report that they sometimes feel demoralised about their work with young children because they spend so much time responding to young children's inappropriate behaviour. This leaves little time for the real work which is relating to, playing with and helping young children learn the skills for living as competent human beings in their community and society. A far more pleasant and constructive option is to find ways in which many commonly occurring behaviour problems may be prevented, which then eliminates the need to respond to such incidents.

Problem prevention begins with care and attention to the environment which has both physical and emotional dimensions (Fields and Boesser, 1994). The environment can be set up in such a way that both appropriate or inappropriate behaviours can be encouraged. Some early childhood professionals mistakenly believe that if a session with a group of young children runs smoothly, it is because the children are normal and well behaved. They often do not understand that when things are running smoothly, it is because the adult in charge has carefully considered the specific environment and group of children as well as her expectations and aims. These factors have been used to plan and create a physical and emotional environment which makes it easier for young children to engage in appropriate behaviour.

There are a number of factors which generally are considered to contribute to creating a preventive approach to discipline and an environment that fosters cooperative and appropriate behaviour in young children. These include, among others, the adults' attitudes to children and each other, the arrangement of the room, the type and timing of experiences offered, the daily routine and opportunities for privacy and sharing. A number of factors which are considered to be essential in problem prevention when working with young children are outlined below.

FACTORS IN THE PHYSICAL ENVIRONMENT

In planning a program for young children, whether it be conducted in a family day carer's home, a child care centre or a kindergarten, early childhood professionals need to examine the physical environment and identify features of that environment which may help promote positive behaviours in young children and those features which may contribute to children engaging in inappropriate behaviours. Once these factors are recognised, it usually is not difficult to make some minor changes to the physical environment which can result in a more harmonious day with and for young children.

Obviously, the environment should be carefully examined for any potential structural hazards and these be modified or eliminated where possible. There should be no need to keep reminding children 'Don't go near the fence, it's too dangerous', 'Stay away from that rocky ledge, you could fall over it' or 'Be careful of the sprinkler system when you're running. You could trip over and hurt yourself'. Even though government building regulations are meant to prevent such problems in early childhood centres, there may be potential hazards in specific centres that have not been recognised or which have developed since an inspection. Early childhood professionals need to ensure that the physical environment is 'child-proofed' (Miller, 1984).

Noise level

In your work with young children, have you ever noticed that, when the environment becomes noisy, some children seem to become disruptive, uncooperative and aggressive? Often this happens at the end of the day when children are getting tired. There is a clear relationship between noise level and inappropriate behaviour. Sometimes early childhood professionals are concentrating on their interactions with one particular child or small group and fail to notice that the noise level has increased slowly to unacceptable levels. When a group of ultimately unruly children finally gains their attention, they respond reactively to this behaviour. By taking care to avoid an escalation of noise, early childhood professionals will avoid problems arising when children cannot cope with noise levels. Early childhood professionals need to be aware of the role noise has in unacceptable behaviour and constantly monitor noise levels in the room. In this way, the need to respond to children's unruly behaviour is eliminated and frayed tempers are saved!

Activity level

In the same way as noise, heightened activity levels in the room appear to be associated with uncooperative, unruly and unacceptable behaviour in some children. When the activity in the room becomes fast, with children moving quickly and excitedly through the room, spending little concentrated time involved in adult initiated activities and more time in their own games, some children themselves become unmanageable and engage in inappropriate behaviour, such as destroying other children's block buildings, upsetting puzzles or punching other children who get in their way. It seems as if these children cannot cope with a physical environment that is too noisy or too active. Such children may require adult intervention in order to help them gain personal control again. Their inappropriate behaviour is perhaps a cry for help. They know that inappropriate behaviour gains adult attention and reaction. Consequently, inappropriate behaviour may be some children's strategy to gain adult assistance to bring an environment in which they are unable to cope back into manageable proportions. Early childhood professionals need to be sensitive to the increasing activity level in the room in order to help prevent discipline incidents from occurring.

Both noise and activity level tend to increase slowly and subtly, with minor increases going unnoticed by adults for some time. It is therefore important to monitor both noise and activity levels at regular intervals so that proactive intervention can take place and eliminate the need for reactive adult intervention later.

The arrangement of the room

Early childhood professionals spend a great deal of time setting up their rooms to make them look attractive and inviting, with areas for large group, small group and individual activities related to their program or curriculum planning. It is important to consider the arrangement of the room in terms of its potential to contribute to young children's inappropriate behaviour. For, example, the area for story time may be set up next to the shelves which hold the musical instruments. The children may not be able to resist the temptation of touching, picking up or making noise with the musical instruments which is very disruptive to storytelling! If the early childhood professional wants children to pay attention and listen to the story, then the physical environment should enable them to do this and not be distracting. Holding the story in another part of the room or changing the shelving arrangements may be the solution to what could be a potentially very frustrating problem for both children and adult.

In the same way, if the block building area is set up next to a door leading to the outdoor area or bathroom, then it is highly likely that problems may occur from children walking or rushing by and knocking the block constructions over. Locating the blocks in an area where they can be protected from passers by is a sensible way of preventing problems from occurring. In addition, it is useful to consider whether certain activities or learning centres are better located nearer to one another rather than being situated in distant parts of the room. If the children use other materials as part of their block building, then it is helpful if these are located within easy reach. The more children move around their constructions, the greater the probability of them being knocked down with the resultant frustration and aggression. The environment should contribute to successful block building rather than act in a way to make it a frustrating experience for young children. Similarly, having the quiet area for privacy or reading located next to the dramatic play, woodwork or water play area is likely to cause problems between children who want to engage in very different activities.

Another common problem with room arrangement is that unintentionally a fast track circuit which encourages a lot of movement by children can be set up. While it is acknowledged that young children find it difficult to be physically quiet for extended periods of time, it is not helpful for children's learning to be in an environment which encourages running or fast movement inside. This is an activity which should be planned for outdoors. On the other hand, the environment should provide for reasonable movement and mobility within the room to enable children to meet their own needs to be physically comfortable.

Early childhood professionals who are aware that the way in which the room is set up can help young children's cooperative and constructive behaviour have fewer demands to intervene in behavioural incidents, which enables them to devote more time to meeting young children's learning needs.

Space

The amount of personal space which early childhood professionals allocate to each child for certain experiences or activities can be another area where behavioural problems can emerge. Different children require different amounts of personal space and this amount can vary from day to day. Some children require more personal space around them in order to feel sufficiently physically and emotionally comfortable. Without sufficient space, these children often find it difficult to concentrate on what they are meant to be involved in. For example, small group finger painting may work well with four children at the table. However, if another child joins that activity, there may not be sufficient personal space for some or all children. This can result in jostling, making more space by elbowing other children or verbal aggression to the newcomer or other group members. The early childhood professional who is aware of children's need for personal space will ensure that there is sufficient space for each participant and set clear limits about the number of children who may participate in the activity at one time.

Personal space can be a large contributor to problems early childhood professionals experience in settling children down to listen to a story. Even if a large area is provided for children to 'sit on the mat', some children will come and sit virtually on top of another child. This usually results in the child whose personal space has been invaded elbowing out at the other child, pushing her away and complaining about the invasion of her territory. If the early childhood professional begins the story without settling the issue of personal space for the group of children, she may find that the story is disrupted continually by the need to respond to children who are unsettled. The continual disruption of the story may frustrate other children who previously had been settled and concentrating. With their concentration broken, they too may begin to engage in unacceptable behaviour such as calling out, moving around or provoking their neighbours with verbal or physical challenges. Group control has been lost by the adult who will need to regain order before story telling can commence again. A far simpler strategy is to check with the group of children before the story is begun if they have enough space to feel comfortable for the story. If some children indicate a need for more space, then they should be given the opportunity to move. A movement rhyme, such as 'I wriggle my . . . head, shoulders, arms etc,' may be helpful for settling children into their space. If it appears that one child is sitting too close to another child, then the early childhood professional could request that the two of them find a bit more space before the story begins. In this way, the early childhood professional can prevent problems from occurring during the story by arranging appropriate space for the time needed for story telling.

Occasionally certain children demonstrate a preference for more distant physical contact with their peers. They do not like other people to come too close to them and prefer a more physically distant interaction. If such a preference is noticed by the early childhood professional, problems which may arise from invasion of the child's personal space may be prevented by asking the child to illustrate how much space they need from others by drawing a circle around them on the floor. The other children can see for themselves the amount of space needed by that particular child which can assist them in understanding how close they can come without that child feeling that her territory has been invaded. Another useful strategy is for children to have their own carpet square which assists with the concrete, visual definition of each other's space.

Preventing problems from occurring by being attentive to the personal space needs of children for specific activities is a relatively easy task for early childhood professionals which can mean that some common behavioural incidents may never eventuate.

Time

Young children tend to need considerably more time to become engaged in and complete their activities than many adults allow. Tension can arise between early childhood professionals and young children if children are not permitted sufficient time in which to undertake activities which are offered or to make a transition into and complete the routines which are part of the daily schedules of early childhood centres. Being sensitive to the time needs of young children can prevent the build up of frustration and subsequent aggression in children who find it difficult to deal with insufficient time allowance. Many early childhood professionals have experienced the need to respond to aggressive outbursts from children who are told to 'hurry up and finish because we have to do something else now'. By allowing sufficient time for individual children and by alerting children, for example, to the fact that 'we will be packing up in ten minutes so you will need to finish what you are doing', behaviour problems associated with them being rushed, having to wait or being over-stimulated can be prevented.

Some children use time as a means of power to control the group and the adults in charge. Have you ever noticed that some children seem to engage in a 'go slow' campaign whenever they are told that the time for this activity is nearly over? It is important for early childhood professionals to be aware of these tactics and to respond to them appropriately. It may be necessary to set limits in the following way: 'Only children who have packed up their equipment (blocks, puzzles, paints, dress-ups or whatever) may go outside'. If a child still persists in 'going slow', the adult may need to set a much tighter limit by indicating that the child has another three minutes to complete her work because at that time it will have to be packed up. At another time, the early childhood professional may need to explain the situation to the child saying something like 'because we are a group in the centre, certain things need to happen at certain times so that everybody is happy. This means that only certain amounts of time can be given for each activity. Next time, I'll help you understand how much time you have got and let you know well in advance when packing up time will be'. In this way, the early childhood professional uses a problem solving approach to the issues of time.

Rest

Part of the physical environment is the way in which the periods of time allocated to certain activities and routines are organised by early childhood professionals. While young children need ample time to pursue their interests in extended, unbroken periods, they also need some quiet, restful time during each day. This has benefits for both children and adults who also need a break from their intensive supervisory and teaching responsibilities in order to re-charge their batteries to work effectively in the afternoon.

While some parents do not wish their child to sleep or rest because they find it difficult to get children to bed and sleep at home in the evening, it is not in the best interests of either the individual child or the group as a whole for them not to have a quiet period during the day. In many early childhood centres, it is not uncommon to encounter weary children, who have run out of energy to cope with the demands of group living, wandering around restlessly and aimlessly. This behaviour often leads to aggressive interactions with other children. When children are tired, they are not in an optimum learning condition and consequently will not gain much from the experiences which are offered. A wiser strategy is to ensure that all children have an opportunity for a rest time which can be, but is not necessarily, a sleep time. Sensitive early childhood professionals will plan to offer activities which can be undertaken quietly by individuals. A rest time in an early childhood centre reduces noise and activity level for an hour or so which gives children a break from the constancy of noise and activity which is an inherent part of group living.

Privacy

One of the unfortunate consequences of children's early involvement in group care and education is the lack of opportunity for privacy. Today's children are the most closely scrutinised and supervised generation of children. Non-familial care demands extra attention to the safety and welfare needs of children. Yet, this need to ensure young children's safety has meant that there is often nowhere that they can go during the day to get away from the watchful eyes of adults or from the interaction demands from other children. Most adults will have experienced the need to get away from people from time to time. Yet, this same need may not be recognised or acknowledged in young children.

Some children can appear to become antisocial following extended periods of interaction with others and engage in behaviours which can disrupt the harmony of the group. Such children need a quiet place, away from other people where they can gain both physical and psychological privacy. This behaviour is normal and is not an indication of any underlying psychological or developmental problem. When these children have had a quiet time by themselves, or perhaps with one special friend, they appear to re-gain the ability to cope with the group situation and are in a better position to learn from the experiences offered.

It is important that children be permitted to have some time by themselves in a place where they feel they are away from the scrutiny and activities of others. This means that early childhood professionals need to arrange the room in such a way that at least one small, cosy and comfortable place for being alone and relatively secluded is provided.

Interruptions

In the same way as insufficient time allowance, interrupting young children unnecessarily during periods when they are concentrating on their work is a certain way of increasing their frustration level and the likelihood of an unacceptable outburst. While it is important for early childhood professionals to give feedback and recognition as children progress with an activity, this needs to be done at appropriate times when interruption to the activity will be minimised. For example, when a child looks up from working on a puzzle, this might be an appropriate time to acknowledge the child's efforts by saying 'John, I've noticed that you've spent a lot of time putting that puzzle together and you've nearly completed it'. However, it would not be helpful to interrupt the child's concentration on the puzzle with a statement such as 'John, Sally wants to begin a puzzle on the table. Would you move all your pieces closer together, please?' It would be more sensible to locate Sally elsewhere so that John does not experience an unnecessary interruption to his concentration.

Certain peer combinations

Young children are very interested in their peers and in developing friendships from an early age. One of the main reasons that parents send young children to group care and education settings is that they believe that the experience will assist their children in making friends, developing social relationships and learning social skills (Rodd and Millikan, 1994). However, parents and early childhood professionals know from experience that not all peer relationships are constructive.

When certain children play together, they can engage in behaviour which neither of them would consider participating in if they were by themselves. It appears that the partnership gives each of the children a certain bravado to flout rules, test limits, challenge adult authority and generally act in an uncooperative and obnoxious way. Such behaviour can be strengthened because it can gain the attention and even admiration of peers who may enjoy vicariously the antics of rebels. Such inappropriate behaviour which arises from specific peer combinations does not facilitate optimum learning conditions for either the individuals concerned or the group and can make the adults' work with young children very tiresome.

If it becomes obvious that certain peer combinations are associated with displays of inappropriate behaviour, the alert early childhood professional will structure the peer combination to avoid such a problem. For example, when John and Simon sit together at lunch time, there appears to be a lot of food spilt on the table, a lot of raucous laughter and perhaps unattractive eating behaviour, such as dribbling food, spitting it out or playing with scraps on the table. This elicits continued reprimands from the adult who is supervising the table but results in little change to the children's behaviour. These behaviours only seem to occur when the two children are together. If one is absent or if they sit at different tables, the lunch time routine runs more smoothly. When the early childhood professional structures the situation by separating the children, sitting them at different tables with other groups of children, the unwanted behaviour does not occur. In this way, the problem is prevented. Similarly, if Jane and Anna sit together on the mat for story time, there seems to be a lot of giggling, whispering and rejection of advances from other peers. By merely separating these two children during story time, such behaviours cease to be displayed, freeing the early childhood professional from the need to monitor and frequently intervene in their behaviour.

Some early childhood professionals will argue that they do not feel comfortable with separating friends. However, it is not suggested that such peer combinations are never permitted to play, eat or interact together. There are many times in an early childhood program where spontaneous peer combinations can be formed. Some of these are appropriate and some inappropriate. The early childhood professional will structure the peer combination when the needs of specific situations present themselves, such as at lunch time or when an extended period of concentration is demanded from the children. Children still will have sufficient opportunities to interact with the peers of their choice at other more appropriate times during the day. If the peer combination continues to encourage unacceptable behaviour, then other forms of intervention may be called for, such as setting limits, social skills training and logical consequences.

As young children develop, the peer group becomes an important and powerful determinant of their behaviour. Early childhood professionals need to learn to analyse peer dynamics and find ways to make the peer group assist them in encouraging rather than hindering appropriate behaviour by young children.

THE EMOTIONAL ENVIRONMENT

While few early childhood professionals would behave intention-ally in a way that would deliberately encourage inappropriate behaviour in young children, it is possible to act in ways that communicate unconscious but subtle messages to children which are better not sent. When young children feel good about them-selves, they are more likely to engage in positive behaviour than if they feel de-valued and incompetent. Chapter 3 on self esteem explains the relationship between feeling good about oneself and the willingness to engage in appropriate behaviour. If young children's emotional needs for security, respect, independence, recognition and relationship are not met, their emotional frustration can lead to displays of unacceptable behaviour in the early childhood centre.

Security

Children who feel accepted and valued for who they are and who are brought up in an environment which is educative rather than punitive are more likely to feel confident, competent and a part of the group. If they feel that they are being treated fairly and consistently, they are more likely to accept adult management in relation to inappropriate behaviour. Even young children appear to be able to sense that the adult who structures the environment reasonably and who responds predictably to their behaviour does so out of a wish to protect, nurture and guide them. Such an adult orientation provides an emotionally secure basis from which young children can learn and flourish. Young children who do not feel a sense of security are more likely to engage in behaviours designed to keep the adult involved and close to them. Such behaviours are inappropriate in a group situation because they monopolise the adult and do not give the early childhood professional freedom to respond to the group as well as to the other children individually.

Respect

Early childhood professionals usually expect young children to respect their wishes, meet their expectations and generally go along with what they want. It is important to remember that if you want to gain respect, then you also need to give respect. It is important for young children and adults to learn to respect each other and attempt to understand each other's point of view. As young children grow and develop, they want to be listened to and understood, to be acknowledged and to have some say in the decisions which affect their lives. Early childhood professionals who are power-assertive and autocratic tend to encourage rebelliousness on the part of young children (Fields and Boesser, 1994). They set up power struggles with young children by giving ultimatums and expecting children to obey blindly. Adults rarely win such situations! They tend to be defeated in battles of will which can sometimes escalate into a wish to 'get back at' or take revenge on the children involved. Sensitive adults side step such power struggles. They do not set up 'no-win' situations by giving ultimatums. They are prepared to respect young children by sharing the power in terms of offering choices and involving children in decision making and rule making. Such a respectful orientation communicates to children that you value their ideas and point of view, are willing to go along with their wishes at times and that adult wishes and perspectives are not more important than those of children. Young children who feel respected are more likely to engage in cooperative behaviour, thus decreasing the early childhood professional's need to be reactive to undesirable behavioural displays.

Independence

Usually young children do not behave deliberately in ways that they know upset adults. It is far more probable that they want to live and play in a constructive and harmonious learning environment. However, as they grow up, they have an increasing need to be independent, to 'do it myself'. Some early childhood professionals are reluctant to allow children developmentally appropriate independence for a range of reasons. For example, they may not believe that the child is physically or intellectually capable of completing an activity such as carrying a tray of cups into the kitchen. They may not want to share what they consider to be their role, such as permitting children to answer each other's questions or to show another child how to put a difficult piece of the puzzle in. Again, they may feel that 'if you want it done properly, then you have to do it yourself', that is, they do not trust that the child's efforts to clean the paint from the table will meet their standards. They may be unwilling to allow toddlers to engage in feeding themselves because they 'take too much time and make too much mess'.

When early childhood professionals communicate openly or even more subtly such expectations, they are depriving young children of the opportunity to fulfil their emotional need to be independent and to develop competence. Young children's behaviour tends to be consistent with adult expectations. If early childhood professionals communicate to children that they have faith in their ability to handle the situation competently, then children are more likely to rise to the occasion. If children's abilities are underestimated or ignored, then children will find some other, often undesirable, behaviour to demonstrate their independence to adults. It is far more profitable for early childhood professionals to engage children in constructive, developmentally appropriate, independent behaviours and avoid the need to respond to children's inappropriate attempts to be independent.

Recognition

To learn to trust the adults and peers that a child spends her day with, each child needs to be provided with affection, understanding and attention on an individual basis each day. In a group care and education situation, it is often difficult for the early childhood professional to attend responsively to the needs of each individual child at meaningful and relevant times. Sometimes, early childhood professionals fall into the trap of using comparison and competition as a way of recognising or motivating children. Both comparison and competition tend to make children feel bad about themselves and are associated with a diminished sense of self esteem. However, if children do not feel that they are noticed, they can feel discouraged, insignificant, disconnected from the group and even rejected. Research evidence indicates that children who feel important and valued and who have a warm, positive relationship with the early childhood professional tend to behave in accordance with the adult's expectations and desires (Marion, 1991). It is therefore in the best interests of the child and the early childhood professional to develop a relationship and pattern of interaction which encourages the child to engage in desirable behaviours.

To communicate recognition to a child, it is important to use the child's name frequently, to offer the child periods of regular attention at appropriate times and to converse naturally about the child's activities, interests and family. It is also helpful where possible to set aside a special time, say once a week, for a one-to-one interaction with each child where the adult can relate more intimately with the child. In addition, recognising children's efforts and successes is also a way, but not the only way, of communicating to children that they are important and valued members of the group.

There are many ways in which early childhood professionals can communicate that they recognise each child as an individual and as part of the group, thereby creating a personal relationship which will foster children's willingness to be cooperative in the early childhood centre.

Relationship

Today's young children spend many long hours in centre-based child care. It has been estimated that some children who enter group care at the age of six weeks and leave when they go to primary school spend as many as 12 500 hours in early childhood care and education centres! This is nearly as long as the time they will spend in both primary and secondary school combined. It is essential then that these children's emotional need to build meaningful and satisfying relationships with the people that they spend a great deal of time with is fulfilled. Given the comparatively small amount of time some children spend with their parents and family, early childhood centres have become the arenas where young children learn to relate to other people, both children and adults. They need to be with adults who are willing to form warm, positive, friendly relationships with them because this is where and how they will learn the skills to establish and maintain all future relationships.

A genuine relationship, as opposed to an artificial one, offers the child an opportunity for friendship, intimacy, sharing and problem solving as well as an opportunity to learn to see and appreciate other people's point of view, to compromise and to work out disagreements and disputes in mutually satisfying ways. Unfortunately, some parents are threatened by their child becoming friendly with the early childhood professional and feel that this relationship may become more significant than the parent–child bond. It is usually only in parent–child relationships where extreme emotional deprivation is evident that might this become the case. The parent–child bond will be the primary and most significant bond for most children. Alternatively, some early childhood professionals are fearful of becoming too attached to young children because they know that the children will eventually leave to go to other centres or school and do not want the children to face the pain of separation. However, learning to deal with separation is an unavoidable part of emotional development that all human beings have to learn at some stage. An early childhood professional who is trained in child development will be able to assist children through such an event and strengthen the child's understanding of and ability to deal with such situations in the future. Depriving children of a relationship in order to prevent the pain of separation is not helpful and ultimately not in the best interests of the child.

A genuine relationship with at least one adult in an early childhood centre is a legitimate right for young children. When children feel that they are cared about and care for someone special, they are more likely to engage in behaviours which meet the expectations and wishes of that person. A warm, accepting relationship is part of an optimum learning environment. Children are better prepared to learn and learn better when they feel cared for. Therefore, developing a special relationship with young children is another way that early childhood professionals can take an educative approach to behaviour management and prevent behaviour problems from occurring.

THE CURRICULUM

Feelings of success and frustration in terms of handling the program or curriculum can also be related to young children's behaviour. If an early childhood professional offers children activities which are either too difficult or not sufficiently challenging, children may engage in inappropriate behaviour out of boredom or frustration. It is certainly a challenge for early childhood professionals to offer today's diverse groups of children, with their varying developmental ranges, the most appropriate curriculum at the appropriate developmental level. However, observation of young children reveals that inadequate programming or curriculum design is a determinant of children's behaviour. It is essential that early childhood professionals carefully consider the curriculum in terms of individual and group needs. Children need the opportunity to challenge themselves and to have the opportunity to experience success in the majority of cases. When bored or frustrated children are offered a curriculum suitable for their developmental level, behaviour problems often disappear.

A developmentally appropriate curriculum also has the advantage of meeting young children's emotional needs for security, respect, independence, recognition and relationship. Such a curriculum will provide for a wide range of abilities and will be responsive to young children's growth, development and widening interests.

To conclude, in attempting to prevent behaviour problems from occurring, early childhood professionals need to regularly examine both the physical and emotional environment of their centres in order to identify areas where changes can be made. As well as structuring the environment to prevent problems from occurring, it is also essential to have clear expectations about aims, what behaviours are acceptable and unacceptable and to communicate clear guidelines about behaviour to children. It is important to remember that young children are still learning the norms and rules of their family, culture, community and society and therefore it is the early childhood professional's role to teach, guide and educate as well as to anticipate and intervene in order to prevent problems from occurring.

7

PUNISHMENT AND ITS EFFECTS ON YOUNG CHILDREN

Many adults believe that punishment, or the power-assertive approach to behaviour management, is the most effective way to teach children what is expected of them. This belief is derived from traditional cultural attitudes to child rearing as well as from early childhood professionals' own experience as children. How often do we hear the words 'That's the way I was brought up and it didn't hurt me!' However, many writers on the subject of behaviour management do not recognise punishment as a form of discipline (Webb, 1989).

What is punishment? Broadly defined, punishment is anything that a child finds aversive or unpleasant. Punishment is administered by another person (usually an adult or older child) with the intention of causing an aversive or unpleasant experience for the child. Punishment can mean administering something unpleasant, such as a smack, a pinch, a threatening look, a threatening remark or imposing an unpleasant experience such as being confined to a bedroom, being forced to eat certain foods or being forced to stand in the corner. Punishment also can mean removing something that the child is enjoying, finds pleasant or is of value to the child. Examples of this form of punishment include withdrawing privileges such as an allowance, favourite toys, television, dessert at the end of a meal or sending friends home in the middle of a game.

It is important to understand that what one child finds aversive or unpleasant may not be experienced as such by another child. The degree to which children experience punishment as such also differs between individual children. Some children experience a 'look' as intimidating whereas other children are unaffected by a 'look'. Therefore, it is unwise to generalise about the individual effects of punishment. The fact that 'it didn't hurt me' might be one person's experience of punishment does not mean that this will be other people's.

Personal observations of the effects of punishment on children lead many early childhood professionals to draw the conclusion that punishment indeed does work. It often seems that, only when punishment is administered, do children change their behaviour and comply with adult demands. However, the literature (Rodd and Holland, 1990) has shown that punishment works but only in the short term. Therefore, it does not meet the professional goals for responding to children's behaviour which have been discussed in Chapter 5.

More importantly, punishment has been found to produce detrimental side effects for children which can influence the way children behave and interact as adults (Honig, 1985). Early childhood professionals are responsible for nurturing children's development and well being so that they will develop into socially and culturally acceptable adults. It is contrary to the early child hood professionals' goals for working with children to engage in practices which are detrimental to children's development and well being.

When the effects of punishment on children and their development become familiar to early childhood professionals, the necessity to acquire other ways of guiding and disciplining young children becomes evident. Some of the effects of punishment are described below.

1 Punishment suppresses behaviour but it does not eliminate it

When responding to children's behaviour, there are times when the adult's goal is to eliminate or get rid of the behaviour. For example, swearing is a behaviour which many parents and early childhood professionals wish to eliminate from children's behavioural repertoire. The goal usually is not merely to suppress the behaviour because such a behaviour is deemed inappropriate in the majority, if not all, situations. Spitting, hitting or hurting other people, biting and destroying property are other examples of behaviours where the aim is to eliminate rather than to merely suppress the behaviour. Consequently, where the goal of behaviour management is elimination of undesirable behaviour, punishment is not an effective strategy to use.

2 Punishment suppresses behaviour usually only in the presence of the punisher

It does not take a great deal of experience in working with young children to gain the insight that they tend to do what is expected or what the early childhood professional wants them to do when she is in the room. Many of us have had the experience of stating a rule or reprimanding children, only to find when we leave the room, have their attention diverted elsewhere or are out of sight, that the children resume the forbidden activity. Most adults can remember times when they acted in such a way as children, that is, only complied with adult expectations when the adult was in sight or watching them. In fact, many adults take this attitude when they are driving, that is, only obey the road rules when the police are in the vicinity! The reason why adults do this is to avoid possible punishment, that is, a fine. Children behave in this way for exactly the same reason. While they might wish to continue with what they were doing, they do not want to risk a punishment. So, they choose not to engage in that particular behaviour in the presence of a potential punisher.

However, early childhood professionals are not police! The goal of guiding children's behaviour is not to teach children to observe rules and behave appropriately because an adult is in the room or is watching children in order to 'catch them being naughty'. This encourages avoidance behaviour in children, that is, compliance with adult expectations only to avoid punishment. While the presence of an adult may act as a cue or prompt to remind children of what is expected, early childhood professionals have specific goals or reasons for why they require certain behaviour and why they will not permit other behaviours. They have a responsibility to help children learn the reasons why certain behaviours are expected so that children can learn to make informed decisions about their own behaviour.

3 Punishment teaches children to associate punishment with the punisher not with their behaviour

An interesting outcome of punishment is that children do not appear to associate punishment with their behaviour. Rather, they associate punishment with the person who administered the punishment (Gordon, 1974). This means that if adults are attempting to eliminate an inappropriate behaviour, for example swearing, by using punishment (such as removing the child from the group or severely reprimanding the child), it is unlikely that the child will make the connection between their behaviour and what they have encountered from the adult. She is more likely to think that the adult is mean, nasty and a witch! The child who has been punished may begin to dislike the adult. So, the punishment does not have an impact upon the child's behaviour but does have an unintended, negative impact on the relationship between the adult and the child (Gordon, 1971).

Many early childhood professionals report that they are dealing with persistently disobedient and non-compliant children. When they outline the strategies that they are using to deal with the behaviour, it becomes clear why children's inappropriate behaviours are persistent. The adults, probably unintentionally, have resorted to the use of punitive techniques with these children. It is often difficult to remember, especially in the heat of the moment, that children do not tend to connect the punishment with their behaviour. However, as the early childhood professional becomes more frustrated with the child's lack of responsiveness to her efforts, the relationship with the child can begin to deteriorate, particularly if the child now perceives the adult as out to make her life miserable!

If the child begins to dislike the early childhood professional because of the behaviour management strategies employed, the child may start to become apprehensive about coming to the preschool, child care centre or the family day carer's home. Refusal to go to creche or preschool is a matter of concern for many parents who may be feeling guilty about using child care and early educational services for their children. If children tell their parents that the early childhood professional has been mean to them, that they don't like her or that they were not allowed to join in, parents naturally will become very concerned. The anxiety that many parents experience about having their child in child care or preschool often is ameliorated by the warm, caring relationship that is observed between child and early childhood professional by the parent. The disruption to this relationship that can be caused by the use of punitive techniques is likely to be of extreme concern to parents who may look for an alternative care or educational arrangement for the child.

Early childhood professionals have a dual responsibility: to establish and maintain a positive relationship with each child as well as helping children learn how to behave in socially and culturally acceptable ways. Punishment does not assist adults working in early childhood settings to meet either of these responsibilities.

4 Punishment produces emotional side effects which lower children's self-esteem

The potential problem of the child beginning to dislike the person who administers the punishment has been discussed under the previous point. However, punishment also can lead to children not liking themselves.

Young children need to feel that they are liked, valued and regarded as competent by others in the environments in which they spend their time. If early childhood professionals adopt a punitive attitude to children, they convey a message which may be either covert and subtle through gestures, facial expression and tone of voice or overt and obvious in the language and activities employed. The message is 'I do not like you, I do not value you and I do not think that you are capable'. Children are highly attuned to such messages and tend to interpret perceived negative or hostile responses from early childhood professionals in personal terms. They begin to think that they are not worthwhile or significant and consequently may begin to act in such a way.

If early childhood professionals label children as lazy, stubborn, disobedient, rude, insolent, hopeless or whatever, children incorporate these adult reflections into their self concept, their perceptions of themselves. If they treat children in a hostile, harsh and demeaning manner or with ridicule, children perceive themselves as 'bad', unworthy and even unlovable. These too are incorporated into the self concept. As children come to understand what characteristics are valued and scorned by society, they begin to evaluate their own characteristics and attributes. If early childhood professionals have communicated to children through behaviour management techniques that they possess qualities not valued by society, they will not value themselves. Their self concept will be lowered.

Early childhood professionals have a responsibility to interact with children in ways that foster children's positive self concept and enhance children's sense of worth. Because feedback from adults is crucial in these areas, it is important that early childhood professionals employ behaviour management strategies that do not diminish children's self concept and self esteem.

5 Punishment does not provide guidance to appropriate behaviour for children

When adults punish children, they usually focus upon what behaviours they do not want rather than on what they would find acceptable in the situation. Early childhood professionals and parents have been heard to tell children 'Stop it!', 'No, don't do that!', 'Get away from there' and other such directives. While the early childhood professional may be clear about what she wants to happen, it is erroneous to assume that children think in the same way as adults do. Adults need to think not only about what they want children to stop doing but also about what they want children to do instead. For example, John (aged 3) is spooning his vegetables out of the bowl onto the table at lunch time. The early childhood professional reprimands John in a harsh voice saying 'Stop that, John. It's disgusting!' What has John learned from this exchange? Only that the adult does not want him to spoon food on to the table. John's interpretation of this message may be that it is not okay to spoon food on to the table but dropping it on to the floor or flinging it at the wall may be all right. John has not been given any clues by the early childhood professional to why the behaviour was unacceptable or what behaviours might have been acceptable. A valuable teaching opportunity has been lost. A more constructive way of dealing with such a situation might be to say 'John, we keep our food in the bowl so it is ready to eat'.

The major role for early childhood professionals in behaviour management of young children is to help children learn what are appropriate and acceptable behaviours in the situations they experience. Punishment only does part of the job. It does not help children learn what to do but only what is not acceptable. It does not help children learn the reasons why the behaviour is unacceptable, only that the adult does not like it.

6 Punishment produces aggression in children

A growing body of research evidence has revealed the strong relationship between punishment and aggression in children (Honig, 1985). Children who are punished usually become angry with the person who has inflicted the punishment upon them. This anger is displaced in an aggressive attack which can be further displaced to an inappropriate person or object. The stereotype of the person who has had a bad day at the office coming home and kicking the cat or slamming the door can be seen to operate with young children. A child who has been punished usually feels hurt and may want to retaliate or take revenge. Given that the punisher is generally older, bigger, stronger and able to hurt the child even more if the child retaliates directly, some children take their anger and hurt out on other children or property. For example, Oliver (aged 5) who had been removed from the activity because he has destroyed another child's collage immediately goes over to the block corner and knocks down Jason's tower. A harsh reprimand results in Oliver running outside where he breaks the branches of a young tree which recently had been planted in the garden. Susy (aged 4) refused to clean up the paint brushes. On being told that she would not be able to participate in the story, she ran to the book corner, chose a book and began to tear pages out of it.

Such examples illustrate the potentially destructive outcome of punishment for individual children, the group and property. Any temptation on the part of early childhood professionals to increase the punishment is likely to result in further aggression from children who generally see punishment as an expression of power by adults.

7 Punishment is not effective unless it is delivered immediately following the behaviour and is consistently applied

One of the difficulties for adults who use punishment is that any delay in administering it weakens its effectiveness. The connection between punishment and behaviour is dependent on the immediate and consistent application of punishment. In day to day interaction with children in an early childhood context, it is not always possible or feasible to respond to children's behaviour immediately. While the presence of parents or other adults should not inhibit appropriate behaviour management strategies being employed, their presence may not provide circumstances in which the early childhood professional has sufficient time to think about how best to respond to an incident. If such a situation should occur, the early childhood professional needs to find an opportunity to respond to the child as soon as possible. Similarly, the early childhood professional may be involved in an activity with another child and not be free to respond. Inappropriate behaviour may go unnoticed because, given the range of demands in a centre, the early childhood professional may be preoccupied with or involved in something else.

Many mothers have used the threat 'Wait until your father gets home. He'll sort you out!' What many mothers do not realise is that the long delay between the child's behaviour and the threatened punishment from the father makes it impossible for the child to make a connection between punishment and their behaviour. By the time the father has arrived home, the child has forgotten what the problem was. The punishment appears to come out of the blue. However, the child may develop very negative feelings about the father who appears to inflict unpleasant experiences on the child in a random manner. Some early childhood professionals have been heard to use this same threat ('Wait until your parents get here, I'll tell them how you've behaved today. They'll make sure you won't do it again') to respond to children's inappropriate behaviour in early childhood centres. This is not only an ineffective practice but it has a negative impact upon children's relationships with their parents. Children can become apprehensive about and fearful of the parents' arrival and reaction to their transgressions. Early childhood professionals have a responsibility to nurture the sometimes fragile relationship between parent and child and need to avoid acting in ways that can sabotage those important bonds.

Because early childhood professionals and children are people, not machines, and because of the enormous demands involved in the job, it is not always possible to be consistent in the administration of punishment. Most adults are reluctant to employ harsh techniques when responding to young children's inappropriate behaviour. They search for explanations (for example, 'He's not normally so difficult, it's because he's tired') and extenuating circumstances (for example, 'Her father's away and she's feeling insecure') to understand the behaviour. They prefer to use 'softer' methods such as talking to, reasoning with and cajoling children. Sometimes, adults choose to ignore behaviours that they previously have reacted strongly to hoping that the child eventually will desist. However, when such methods do not produce the desired effects, frustration can get the better of even the most well intentioned adult. Early childhood professionals have reported anecdotally that they resort to punishment out of desperation and because they know that punishment will have an immediate impact on children's behaviour.

It appears that many adults, including early childhood professionals, vacillate between having reasonable expectations about children's behaviour, being permissive and being punitive with children. How a situation is handled can depend on the adult's stress level, health, time of day or other factors unrelated to the specific incident. Consequently, the administration of punishment can appear to be a random and haphazard event to children and adults alike. Punishment derives its power over children's behaviour from the certainty that it will be delivered. When that certainty is removed, punishment loses its effectiveness.

Many early childhood professionals feel uncomfortable with such a mechanistic approach to behaviour management for young children. They consider the rigid rules for effective punishment to be de-humanising and inappropriate for responding to young children. However, it is important to understand that inappropriate application of what is really a complex behavioural technology can produce unintended and sometimes harmful outcomes for children. If adults choose to use suitably mild punishment with young children, then they need to understand the principles underpinning its effectiveness and apply them accordingly. They need to be aware of the potential for negative outcomes for young children and be able to justify the use of such strategies on the basis of professional values and standards of practice. For early childhood professionals, it is almost impossible to rationalise the use of punishment in terms of professional values and standards of practice. Given that a range of more constructive approaches to behaviour management are available, early childhood professionals are encouraged to become familiar with other management options.

8 Punishment can increase children's desire to persist with a behaviour

If used frequently, punishment can be the impetus for the development of a long and bitter power struggle between an early childhood professional and a child. The child may decide to accept the punishment but not change the offending behaviour. This is particularly evident when a warm, friendly, nurturing relationship no longer exists between the adult and child. For example, the early childhood professional has withdrawn Mary from the block corner because she consistently refused to pack up the blocks. Mary sits isolated from the group with an angry expression on her face. When invited to come back and finish packing up, Mary is non-committal and wanders away to the home corner. Alternatively, Mary may come back with a hostile and defiant attitude, refusing again to do what has been requested for her.

Such examples illustrate certain attitudes that some children develop in relation to punishment. They will accept what the adult inflicts upon them but remain unchanged by the experience. With a defiant look, these children challenge the adult to change their behaviour by communicating two messages: 'You can't make me' and 'You can't stop me'. Many early childhood professionals will have experienced the utter frustration of trying to make a child do something that they refuse to do, such as clean up or pack away. In the same way, experience has shown that it is often impossible to prevent a child from engaging in a behaviour if that child is determined to persist, for example, in acting aggressively or using inappropriate language.

Early childhood professionals understand that it is futile to engage in a power struggle with a young child. The adult rarely wins. Children usually will defeat an adult because the adult generally does not have the time or emotional energy to continue with the struggle. A typical outcome is that the child continues with the unacceptable behaviour, thinking that they can do as they wish. Alternatively, if the adult becomes angry and 'loses her cool', the child also experiences a sense of having defeated the adult and winning. The child's attitude to accepting punishment in order to do what she wants is reinforced.

9 Punishment does not result in the internalisation of rules or self-discipline

One of the essential goals of behaviour management for young children is to assist children to learn and respect the rules of society and to use these rules to make individual decisions about how to behave in situations which confront them. Punishment does not help children learn these skills. It teaches them to obey those in authority, those who are more powerful and those who can inflict unpleasant experiences upon them. Early childhood professionals do not respond to children's behaviour simply to gain obedience and compliance from children. As has been discussed earlier, early childhood professionals do not want those in their care to comply with rules and expectations only to avoid possible punishment from the adults who are present. If this were to be the case, all of us would need the police following us around to make sure that we did the right thing! We would only obey and comply in order to avoid punishment. For children and adults, many decisions about what is the appropriate way to behave have to be made in the absence of other people who can inform us about what to do. The only points of reference are the values and rules of society which can be used to guide and regulate behaviour.

Given the teaching and guiding role that early childhood professionals hold in relation to behaviour management, it is important to understand the limited educational value of punishment. Research evidence indicates that punishment is associated with the lowest levels of moral development in children, little internalisation of rules and poorly developed self discipline (Webb, 1989). Therefore, punishment does not assist early childhood professionals in achieving these aims.

10 Punishment can teach children to misbehave

Although this appears contrary to what is expected from punishment, there is considerable evidence (Sabatino, 1991) to indicate that certain punitive strategies act to increase the probability that children will engage in inappropriate and unacceptable behaviour. This can be a product of the way early childhood professionals use their attention. It is acknowledged widely that adult attention is a very powerful tool in shaping children's behaviour. Adult attention is considered to be a reward for children, that is, children enjoy the attention of adults and will behave in ways they believe will gain that attention.

Learning theory advises adults to use their attention selectively with young children (Charles, 1992). Attention should be given to behaviour that is desired, appropriate and acceptable, for example, helpful, cooperative and task-oriented behaviour. Behaviour which is undesirable, inappropriate and unacceptable should be ignored when it is safe to do so. Some behaviours which fall under this category are whining, swearing, fighting and arguing. However, research has revealed that early childhood professionals, as with parents and other professionals who work with children, tend not to use their attention in these ways. In fact, they tend to do the opposite, that is, ignore appropriate behaviour and give attention to inappropriate behaviour.

Early childhood professionals, in the way in which they use their attention, can unintentionally but effectively teach young children to misbehave. When many adults have been observed in their interactions with young children, it becomes evident that they are more concerned with inappropriate behaviour than appropriate behaviour. Early childhood professionals are watchful for inappropriate behaviour (often for reasons of safety and security) and respond to such behaviour quickly and frequently. On the other hand, appropriate behaviours which children might exhibit sometimes appear to go unnoticed by adults. This is often because early childhood professionals erroneously believe that their attention might disrupt the constructive activity that the child is engaged in. Children learn very quickly that, if you want adult attention, the sure way to obtain it is to engage in some inappropriate behaviour. Appropriate behaviour may or may not be attended to.

Early childhood professionals have the responsibility for teaching young children what is acceptable and appropriate as well as what is unacceptable and inappropriate. Children need feedback from adults concerning their appropriate behaviour meeting adult expectations. Early childhood professionals need to ensure that they are not using their attention in ways that encourage children to misbehave.

11 Punishment models power-assertive ways of solving interpersonal problems

Many of the inappropriate behaviours young children engage in are to do with learning how to relate to other people, both peers and adults. Problems of sharing, turn taking, fairness and respecting others' space, time, opinions and property dominate the lives of young children. Children learn methods of solving these problems by observing what other people do and the effects of the strategies. Early childhood professionals can demonstrate both cooperative and power-assertive methods of solving interpersonal problems. Cooperative methods of solving problems are based upon notions of mutual respect, equality, shared responsibility and a win–win perspective. Power-assertive methods of problem solving are based upon notions of superiority of one person over another.

Young children appear to have a natural tendency to respond aggressively to perceived threats. Through sensitive adult guidance, this tendency is modified into an assertive rather than aggressive orientation where children learn to assert their rights without impacting upon the rights and self esteem of others. However, where young children are exposed to adults who use power and aggression to solve interpersonal problems, they learn that power and aggression are effective and legitimate for meeting your own needs. Punishment is an assertion of power by one person over another, an expression of one person's attitude of superiority over an inferior other and an expression of lack of respect for the other person. Considerable evidence exists which indicates that children who observe adults employing the power-assertive strategies of punishment are likely to engage themselves in power-assertive behaviour with other children (Berk, 1991). This tendency also has been documented in young children's play with dolls and other toys.

Early childhood professionals need to be aware of the power-assertive aspect of punishment and consider what the use of such techniques teaches young children about interpersonal relationships and interaction.

12 Punishment is children's first experience of violence

Unfortunately, the first time most children experience the use of hurtful physical force in relation to their behaviour is by their most intimate relative—their parent. While corporal punishment is banned in care and educational settings in almost every state and territory in Australia and in some other countries, a recent study (*Times Educational Supplement,* 15 September 1995) reported that the overwhelming majority of Australian parents believed that it is appropriate to strike children if they warrant it. The parents in the study (which was commissioned by the National Child Protection Council) believed that every parent has the right to discipline children in any way they see fit, including using a ruler, leather strap or wooden spoon to hit children. Despite such evidence concerning parental attitudes, anecdotal reports by parents of young children reveal the surprise, shock and guilt experienced following an incident in which they actually slapped, hit, shook, pinched or bit their beloved child. However, the frustration experienced by many adults concerning the behaviour of young children is considerable and appears to provoke intense emotional reactions in otherwise sane, sensible and emotionally stable people. Most parents would argue that they punished the child for 'her own good' or because 'I'd tried everything else—there was nothing left but to smack him'. While such explanations might help relieve the guilt experienced by adults, the punishment usually does little to address the problem. If it did, adults would not have to continue to use punishment to gain the compliance of small children.

In addition, once adults begin to use punishment with young children, they appear to become de-sensitised to its effects. It does not seem to be such a terrible thing to smack the child after the first time! This de-sensitisation to the use of punishment may explain why adults appear to adopt increasingly severe punishments as children get older as well as the increasing incidence of child abuse.

However, the bottom line is that all societies appear to be becoming more and more violent and de-humanised in their approach to and treatment of fellow human beings. It is important to acknowledge that, especially in societies that condone the use of violent forms of behavioural control in intimate relationships, violence increasingly will be regarded as legitimate and used to solve interpersonal and other problems. Members of all societies need to ask whether we are prepared to accept the infliction of violent physical force on children by their protectors and whether the use of punishment by those in loci parentis, such as early childhood professionals, can be tolerated.

In conclusion, many early childhood professionals appear to hold a number of myths about the effectiveness of punishment for controlling young children's behaviour. There appears to be sufficient research information to dispel those myths and to reveal the harm that the continued use of punishment can have on developing children. Because punishment as a means of behavioural control is so widely accepted in Western society and its use almost automatic by many of us, it is essential that early childhood professionals fully understand the implications of using punishment with young children. It takes a concerted effort to begin to eliminate punitive responses from our habitual ways of dealing with children and to replace them with more appropriate and constructive techniques. However, in terms of early childhood professionals' moral and ethical responsibility to those under their care, it is essential that this task be given a high priority.

Research evidence (Maccoby, 1988; Sabatino, 1991) has documented the effects of punishment on young children. It is important to understand these effects because these are the reasons that compel early childhood professionals to learn and practice other ways of responding to children's behaviour. In addition, many early childhood professionals report a diminished sense of self esteem themselves when they employ punitive practices with children. It is recognised that punishment often is used when they feel angry or frustrated and have not had the opportunity to think through the situation sufficiently. Once early childhood professionals realise the impact such techniques can have upon children and their development as well as themselves, it becomes professionally unethical to engage in such practices. Clyde and Rodd (1989) found that the use of practices that were potentially harmful for children were considered by a large number of the members of the early childhood field to be unprofessional. It was the second greatest concern after identifying and handling suspected child abuse and neglect. When early childhood professionals find that other strategies may not be as immediate as punishment in their impact upon behaviour, or when they feel less confident about their skill to use alternative techniques, it is important to review the effects of punishment. This can give the early childhood professionals added impetus required to put punishment aside and persist with other more positive approaches.

8

COMMUNICATING WITH YOUNG CHILDREN

Because behaviour management is based on the relationship between early childhood professionals and children, communication is one of the key elements to managing young children's behaviour. The language that is used with children by early childhood professionals and the way in which they speak to children about their behaviour are important aspects of helping children learn what is expected of them in the situation. Communication is the basis of an inductive reasoning approach to behaviour management—an approach which is considered to have many advantages for helping young children to develop empathic relationships and self control and to become self disciplined. The foundation for successful relationships between early childhood professionals and children is continuing communication which is based on firmness and respect. These two elements contribute to both early childhood professionals' and children's dignity in the relationship and foster understanding of each other's position in the situation.

There is a certain style of communication which early childhood professionals need to adopt in order to maximise the effectiveness of their interaction with young children. First, it is essential to establish and maintain eye contact with the child. Eye contact is not staring or 'eye-balling' but rather making non-verbal contact by looking at a person generally about their head and shoulders. There is little point in trying to get a message across to a child or group of children if they are not aware that you are trying to communicate with them and you won't know that unless you are actually looking at them. The only way that early childhood professionals can be sure that they have the attention of young children is to engage eye contact. In this way, they can gauge the effect of the message on the child and modify the message if need be. If a child is not looking generally at the early childhood professional's face, it is important to tell her that she needs to look at you. Saying something like 'I can't tell if you are listening to me if you are not looking at me. I need you to look at me when I am speaking to you' can prompt a child to establish eye contact.

However, there are cultural differences in regard to eye contact which need to be considered. In a range of cultures, such as some Asian cultures and Aboriginal cultures, it is considered rude and disrespectful for children to look directly at adults. Early childhood professionals need to be sensitive to cultural norms in relation to eye contact but, as a general rule, it is unwise to begin talking to a child about her behaviour or an incident until eye contact has been established.

Second, early childhood professionals need to control their voices and use a pleasant but firm tone of voice when talking to children. When they raise their voices in frustration or anger, they are communicating a very clear message to children that they have lost control of the situation and can restore control only through intimidation and fear. When young children are frightened or anxious about what an early childhood professional might do in response to their behaviour, their heightened emotions decrease their potential for learning from the situation. Therefore, an angry, loud tone of voice does not help early childhood professionals achieve one of the aims of discipline, that is, assisting young children to learn more appropriate behaviour in the situation.

Third, it is recommended that early childhood professionals communicate with children using their voice at normal volume, rather than shouting and yelling. If a child is at a distance in which it is difficult to communicate, the early childhood professional needs to move over to the child so that appropriate interpersonal communication is possible. Moving closer to the child also communicates an interest in and involvement with the child and her behaviour. It is respectful to be in reasonably close proximity to the person with whom you wish to talk. Shouting and talking in a loud, harsh voice is physically demanding and contributes to increases in adults' stress levels. It is therefore not in the early childhood professional's or the children's best interests to be in an environment where order is maintained by loud, emotionally aroused and stressed adults. A calm, even, matter-of-fact tone of voice can help maintain a friendly and harmonious atmosphere for all concerned.

Fourth, it is important for early childhood professionals to reinforce their verbal communication to children by using appropriate non-verbal communication. Research suggests that nearly 80% of a message is contained in body language and tone of voice (Feldman, 1990). Body language refers to the non-verbal ways that human beings communicate with one another, such as with gestures, facial expression, posture, tone of voice and speed of talking. If you are pleased with a child's behaviour, you need to look as if you are pleased while you tell the child specifically what has pleased you. If you disapprove of certain behaviour, your body as well as your voice needs to convey that message. It is most confusing for children if early childhood professionals say one thing verbally and communicate another message non-verbally. In such circumstances, children, in the same way as adults do, focus on the non-verbal message as being the true message.

There are many instances where children exhibit behaviour which is socially unacceptable but which early childhood professionals also find humorous. For example, aggressive superhero play which is an excellent portrayal of the character, the use of swear words in an adult-like style or reciprocal aggression to a bully in the group. In the same way, early childhood professionals sometimes look bored, uninterested or distracted when communicating approval about a child's behaviour, such as, a child climbing to the top of the slide or a child showing her latest painting. However, if an early childhood professional really wants to communicate approval or disapproval, it is important that both the verbal and the non-verbal message to young children be congruent and consistent.

Finally, many early childhood professionals make the mistake of thinking that communication involves only talking to a child. In fact, effective communication involves more listening than it does talking. Listening is an important tool for developing respectful relationships and for understanding the other person's point of view.

Listening is a skill which needs to be developed and practised by most people. Most of us simply 'hear' as opposed to listening which demands energy and active involvement with the other person. Many of us are unable to listen to other adults, let alone children who we regard as having little worthwhile to offer. In early childhood contexts, listening to young children is essential in order to help them learn appropriate communication styles and ways of relating to others. Many young children do not know how to listen because they themselves have not been listened to. Early childhood professionals who can listen properly act as role models for children who need to learn how to listen as part of communicating.

Listening, sometimes called active listening, involves getting down to the child's level by bending your knees, sitting on a low chair or sitting the child in a chair to bring her up to your level. This permits appropriate eye contact to be established and communicates a certain equality which is part of a respectful relationship. Next, make an 'act of will' to give the child your full attention, ignoring other distractions in the environment. If the room is too noisy or active, it might be helpful to move to a quieter, less distracting area where it is possible to devote your full attention to what the child is saying. Finally, listen beyond the actual words that the child is saying and try to understand what meaning she is trying to convey. Young children's language abilities are developing but many need assistance from early childhood professionals to express what they are trying to get across. It is sometimes helpful to repeat what you think the child is saying or means to say to the child in order to clarify the message. She will tell you if you are wrong. When early childhood professionals listen effectively, they do not interrupt, talk a lot or take over. Rather, they provide appropriate non-verbal encouragement to the child, such as smiles, nods, uh-huhs, ask minimal clarifying questions, provide assistance with the expression of concepts and ideas if necessary and wait until the child is finished before replying.

The use of a positive, relaxed but firm communication style by early childhood professionals helps children understand that adults have their best interests at heart, will protect them if they themselves are unable to handle certain situations and are predictable and consistent when it comes to discussing behavioural incidents.

As well as adopting an appropriate style of communication, there are a number of principles which will enable adults in early childhood settings to communicate more effectively with young children.

1 Communicate your expectations in a positive manner

Because young children are learning what the expectations are in any given situation, it is important to communicate these in a simple and clear style. Many early childhood professionals make the mistake of telling children what they don't want them to do, for example, saying 'Don't shovel the sand out of the sand pit!', 'Get your feet off the table!', 'Stop painting on the wall!' or 'Don't pull Sarah's hair!'. This type of communication only gives children half the message, that is, what you do not want children to do. However, young children are not mind readers. They do not necessarily know what else it is that they might do instead that adults will approve of. Many of us have had the experience of telling a young child what not to do, only to find that they choose another way of behaving which is equally or even more unacceptable! For example, a child might stop shovelling the sand out of the sand pit and decide to throw it at another child. Or a child might take her feet off the table and sit on it instead. A child might be very creative and paint on the floor rather than the wall. And it might be just as satisfying to pull Jason's hair as it is to pull Sarah's!

Therefore, it is essential for early childhood professionals to consider what specific behaviour they want young children to engage in before anything is said. Do you want the child to shovel sand into the middle of the sand pit? Do you want the child to shovel it into a bucket or tip truck? Do you want the child to keep her feet on the floor? Do you want the child to paint on the paper at the easel or on the paper on the table? Do you want the child to become involved in a constructive activity such as building a tower with blocks rather than pulling another child's hair?

It is more helpful for children when early childhood professionals communicate their wishes positively because this type of communication provides guidelines and sets limits which help young children make more appropriate choices about their behaviour. Consequently, early childhood professionals who phrase their wishes and expectations in a positive style are more likely to obtain the desired behaviour from young children. The following examples show how expectations can be communicated positively:

> 'Wong, I want the sand to stay in the sand pit, so I want you to shovel it into the middle please.'
>
> 'Eleanor, please put your feet on the floor and sit in a chair when you are at the table.'
>
> 'I'd prefer it if you painted on the paper at the easel Giovanni, not on the wall.'
>
> 'Rebecca, I want you to come over here with me and help us build a tower for this castle.'

This type of matter-of-fact communication provides the advantage of keeping the atmosphere in the group pleasant and is likely to foster a more cooperative attitude on the part of the children than is an angry or harsh command. When children hear early childhood professionals talk to them in a hostile, threatening manner, they often become defensive and try to protect themselves by retaliating in a hostile manner too. So it is essential for early childhood professionals to keep their tone of voice firm but friendly and unemotional. In this way, early childhood professionals will communicate to young children that they are confident about what they expect from children and that the children will modify their behaviour in terms of the adult's wishes.

2 Communicate your expectations simply

In their efforts to help young children understand why adults want certain types of behaviour, many early childhood professionals make the mistake of going into lengthy and complicated explanations of why they want what they want. Because early childhood professionals want to help children learn social norms and expectations, we believe that it is important to provide children with the reasons for our wishes. This is an important aspect of the teaching role in guidance and discipline. However, early childhood professionals can confuse and bore children with long and detailed explanations about behavioural requirements. Many of us will have seen parents of young children engaging in a serious and logical explanation of why their child cannot have that packet of biscuits at the supermarket and have observed the results. A child who hears a sanctimonious tone of voice tends to switch off and decide that throwing a tantrum might be a more effective and faster way of getting what she wants. In a professional situation, it is important not to make this mistake.

Early childhood professionals who are effective in managing children's behaviour use short, simple and clear statements about their expectations in language that young children understand. In other words, they say what they mean and mean what they say! In the above example, in a calm and confident tone of voice, the parent might say to the child 'I am not buying any biscuits today' and quickly move towards the place where the next item is to be picked up. It is important not to enter into any further debate or argument with the child and the best way of avoiding this pitfall is to move quickly to a non-contentious activity or area.

Examples of other clear and concise statements are:

'Children, I need you to sit down before I can begin the story, please.'

'We're going outside. If you wish to join us, please put your hats on now.'

'Please choose a chair and sit down at the table for your snack, Helmut.'

'I want you to sit next to me while we listen to the music, Amanda.'

These short, simple statements are more likely to be understood by young children whose concentration span and ability to comprehend long and involved communications are limited. Again, because the expectations are stated in a positive and confident manner, there is a greater chance of cooperation and less likelihood that children will perceive an opportunity to argue with the adults. However, early childhood professionals must refrain from commencing the activity until the desired behaviour is obtained from the child or group of children. If you begin the story without the children sitting down, go outside without everyone having their hats on, permit a child who is not sitting at the table to have a snack or begin the music without Amanda sitting next to you, the children will learn that you do not mean what you say and that they can do as they please with no consequences for their behaviour. It is not necessary to repeat your expectation more than once. Simply remain calm and quiet and wait! The peer group often has the power to gain cooperation from young children. If not, the use of natural or logical consequences outlined in Chapter 9 can be a powerful teacher in such circumstances.

Because the use of the negative style of phrasing our expectations appears to be ingrained in many early childhood professionals' communication with children, it is easy to respond automatically with these habit-like statements. However, perceptive early childhood professionals will listen to their own communications and salvage the situation by following a negative statement with a positive one. For example, 'Don't tip the water out of the trough' can be followed very quickly by 'I'd prefer it if you used a smaller jug and poured the water into the funnel'. In this way, young children are provided with an opportunity to learn what is regarded as not appropriate and also what the positive expectations are.

3 Give feedback for specific behaviours

Because young children are learning and early childhood professionals are trying to teach them appropriate social and cultural expectations for their behaviour in a range of situations, it is essential that adults let children know specifically the behaviour to which they are referring. The information that early childhood professionals communicate to children about their behaviour provides guidelines, directions and cues about what is and is not regarded as socially and/or culturally acceptable.

Western society tends to be a mistake-oriented society when it comes to informing children about the appropriateness of their behaviour. As such, early childhood professionals often communicate to children in a general way about the unacceptability or inappropriateness of their behaviour. We forget that children also need to know from adults what it is that they did that was acceptable and appropriate. Our tendency to ignore or fail to comment upon appropriate behaviour is not helpful for young children's learning about what is expected from them in the situation. Therefore, adults need to focus upon what the child did that was right as much or even more than focusing in on what she did that was wrong. Because most young children enjoy adult approval, informing and making positive comments to children about specific behaviour which is considered to be acceptable and appropriate is an important technique for strengthening the relationship between the early childhood professional and the child. In addition, it enhances the probability that the child will engage

in that behaviour again and fulfils the early childhood professional's role in helping the child learn.

However, informing and making positive comments to children
about their behaviour needs to be phrased in specific detail.
Communicating a general positive statement, such as 'Good girl'
or 'Good boy' is not particularly helpful for young children. Their
limited capacity for concentration and memory may mean that they
associate your positive comment with another behaviour which
may or may not warrant such positive feedback. For example, the
early childhood professional may wish to communicate to Susan
that her packing up of the dress-ups was very helpful and
consequently say 'Good girl' on observing such behaviour. Unfortunately, just as this comment is passed Susan might decide to
push Jane out of the way. Upon hearing 'Good girl', Susan might
think that it was for pushing Jane out of the home corner! Young
children's developing communication skills mean that there is a
big potential for misunderstanding in such situations. On the other
hand, if the early childhood professional had said something more
specific, such as, 'Thank you for packing up the dress-ups, Susan',
the potential is increased for Susan to understand the exact
behaviour that the positive feedback was meant for.

A similar situation exists when early childhood professionals
criticise children's behaviour. The phrase 'naughty girl' or 'naughty
boy' does little to assist young children to understand why their
behaviour has met with adult disapproval. Indeed, the message
underlying such a communication is that the child, the doer is
disapproved of, rather than the usual intention which is to
communicate that the behaviour, the deed, is the object of adult
disapproval. In giving young children any criticism or negative
feedback, it is essential to separate the child from the behaviour.
This is because young children tend to personalise adults' messages
and come to believe that they themselves are disapproved of, not
valued and not worthwhile. The effects of such negative comments
are to diminish children's self concept and lower their sense of
self esteem. This has been discussed previously in Chapter 3.

To inform children about behaviour which is disapproved of,
it is essential that early childhood professionals describe exactly
what it is that the child did that was unacceptable (that is, the
deed) and to suggest an alternative behaviour which would have
been acceptable. For example, 'Alice, you left the tricycle outside
the door and someone could trip over it. Next time that you use

it, you will need to put it back in the shed where it belongs.'
This type of communication, when said in a calm and firm voice,
will not threaten a child's developing sense of self esteem and
arouse defensive anger and retaliation. Rather, it provides an
opportunity for cooperation and to be successful in meeting the
early childhood professional's expectations on another occasion.

The use of praise ('You've done such a nice painting. I'm
really proud of you.') and criticism ('You haven't cleaned the bench
properly. That is so typical of your carelessness.') is common in
Western society. These techniques are derived from the behavioural
approach to managing children's behaviour, where positive events,
such as praise, which follow the display of a behaviour, are
considered to increase the probability of that behaviour occurring
again. Similarly, negative events, such as criticism, are considered
to decrease the probability of that behaviour being displayed.
Those professionals who follow the Adlerian model consider praise
to be discouraging to children and prefer to use encouragement
which is discussed in detail in Chapter 9. Encouragement is
considered to be different to praise in that it focuses on the process
of behaviour rather than the end product or the individual and is
given for effort and improvement rather than for a 'job well done'.
Praise is regarded by Adlerians as an external reward for 'good
behaviour' which teaches the child that a product or behaviour is
worthless unless it receives praise and that, in order to be
worthwhile and significant, one must behave in ways that meet
the demands, standards and approval of others. It is important for
early childhood professionals to remember this distinction between
praise and encouragement and to be aware of the potential impact
of praise. While praise is a technique used frequently to acknowledge appropriate behaviour in young children, incorporating some
encouraging comments about behaviour which focus upon effort,
improvement, contribution, self evaluation and self satisfaction will
help prevent unacceptable behaviour from occurring and foster
the development of a positive self concept (Charles, 1992).

4 Allow children to express their feelings

When early childhood professionals intervene in children's behaviour, it is not uncommon for children to become upset or
emotional. Sometimes early childhood professionals find it difficult
to accept the intense feelings that young children can express in

such situations. It is not unusual for them to find that their own emotions have become aroused in response to a child's emotional outburst. For example, a child's angry outburst can arouse anger in an adult, just as a child's sadness about being excluded from a game can arouse a sense of sadness in an adult.

Most young children do not fully understand their emotional reactions and the causes of such emotions. They are not skilled at identifying and correctly labelling their feelings. Neither can many youngsters control their emotions once they are aroused. Occasionally, young children are frightened by the force of their own emotions and need adult assistance and support to manage them. When working with young children, early childhood professionals also can be surprised by the depth of their own emotional reactions to children and their behaviour. Working with young children can be an emotionally demanding experience.

It is important for adults to accept young children's feelings as legitimate and valid. When children are expressing their feelings, especially negative ones, early childhood professionals need to listen without denying them or being critical and judgmental. Many children need help to express their feelings appropriately, using language and words rather than physical means. It is more constructive for children to let their feelings out in words than to kick, bite, hit or destroy property. For example, if Joseph exclaims 'I don't like Sam any more. I won't let him play with me', it is pointless to argue 'No you don't! He's your best friend, you always play together.' A more productive approach is to accept the child's feelings with a statement such as 'I can see how you mightn't be feeling like playing with Sam any more today. I'm sure that you'll be friends again soon.'

A common incident with children's emotions is where children inform the early childhood professional who has expressed disapproval about their behaviour that they hate them. Children's statements such as 'I hate you', 'I don't love you any more' and 'You're not my friend' can be hurtful to early childhood professionals who feel that they have put a lot of effort into trying to help and understand a child. Rather than being tempted to retaliate with an equally hurtful retort, the early childhood professional could say 'I understand that you don't like me for stopping that game but I like you. I'm sure we'll be friends tomorrow.' This type of response communicates to the child that the expression of feelings is acceptable, that no permanent damage is done to the relationship by expressing one's feelings and reassures the child that her point of view is acknowledged and respected.

While positive styles and techniques of communication are essential for early childhood professionals to acquire, it must be understood that effective communication takes and needs time. All the skills and strategies available are no substitute for time children can spend with the adults who are part of their daily lives. Early childhood professionals need to plan for opportunities when they can talk and listen to children when things are going well. The development and maintenance of solid relationships depends on regular communication. The bonds built during exchanges in harmonious situations will help ease the tension when the situation is not as comfortable for children and adults alike.

To summarise and review some of the key points in relation to the role of communication in the management of young children's behaviour, it is important that early childhood professionals learn to recognise and avoid what are regarded as negative styles and hence barriers to effective communication. Some of these are (modified from Lerman, 1984):

- Acting and talking in a harsh manner.
- Shouting and yelling.
- Using ridicule, sarcasm and name calling.
- Nagging.
- Humiliating and putting down a child in public and in private.
- Joking about and teasing a child.
- Giving orders and commands.
- Creating conflict with a child.
- Getting into a power struggle or win-lose situation with a child.
- Using physical force or hurtful gestures such as smacks, pushes and pinches.

When adults communicate with children effectively and constructively in discipline situations, they do so by (modified from Lerman, 1984):

- Being empathic, showing understanding and respecting the child's point of view.
- Using a pleasant, calm and normal tone of voice.
- Stating clear, simple, friendly and firm expectations in a positive way.

- Offering appropriate suggestions and alternatives for behaviour.
- Enjoying and verbally appreciating children's appropriate behaviour.
- Expressing feelings, especially anger in an appropriate and constructive manner.
- Using humour and seeing the funny side of the situation to de-fuse the tension.
- Being consistent and predictable in reactions to children's behaviour.
- Using positive, affectionate non-verbal communication such as smiles, nods, hugs, touch and laughter.

In conclusion, early childhood professionals' skills in effective communication plays a large part in managing young children's behaviour. These skills also assist the early childhood professional in her relationships with colleagues, parents and other adults associated with the early childhood centre. It is important to remember that one needs to be aware of one's communicative effectiveness and to regularly monitor one's skill as a communicator. All of us can work to improve our communication skills which in turn helps us deal with the interpersonal problems that are part and parcel of daily life with children.

9

POSITIVE STRATEGIES FOR GUIDING YOUNG CHILDREN'S BEHAVIOUR

The aim of behaviour management is not to punish young children or to make them merely comply, conform and obey in a mechanical way. Rather the goals of behaviour management should be to help children learn to solve social problems constructively (Clewett, 1988) by gradually developing internal controls (Pardeck, 1988) over their behaviour, without sacrificing the ability to spontaneously and freely express themselves. Being overly restrictive and inhibiting children's desire to behave spontaneously because they fear adult reprisal does not produce children who feel good about themselves, who can make appropriate choices in terms of their own needs, the needs of others and the needs of the situation and who are independent and capable. Nor does being overly permissive by setting no reasonable limits and having no reasonable expectations about behaviour. What is needed is a balanced approach where freedom and choice is offered to young children in an ordered, firm and kind environment.

Early childhood professionals need to develop their own way of working with young children in order to:

- Assist children to develop the ability to control their own behaviour, that is, to help them become self disciplined.
- Help children learn and be guided by the rules and expectations that are considered important in their culture, community and society.

This is a lengthy process and its progress is determined to a large degree by young children's developmental levels and limitations. It is not normally until early adolescence, when a child is approximately thirteen, that children can truly internalise rules (Pardeck, 1988; Webb, 1989) and use them to regulate their own behaviour.

There are no magical solutions for obtaining the behaviour that adults want from children. No one technique will work every time for every problem or with every child. However, when early childhood professionals learn to view behaviour management as an educative process and as a teaching opportunity, they are more able to match an appropriate strategy to the child and the problem and consequently be more effective in managing the presenting incident. For early childhood professionals, managing young children's behaviour is a problem to be solved, an aspect of working with young children which presents itself on a daily basis. If one adopts this perspective, then the early childhood professional is freed from the need to be rigid, controlling and self blaming about behavioural incidents which occur. Rather, they are permitted to take a problem solving approach which allows choice, flexibility, risk taking and evaluation of the outcome of the use of a particular strategy. Such an approach reduces the incidence of ad hoc, reactive, habitual and less effective responses in favour of more reflective, responsive, planned, proactive and professional responses. Instead of feeling demoralised about their ability to manage young children's behaviour, early childhood professionals who have adopted a problem solving approach to behaviour management usually report a positive sense of self esteem and a higher degree of job satisfaction.

When choosing a strategy to respond to a behavioural incident, it is essential to consider:

- The child's developmental level.
- Any factors in the child's life which may be affecting current behaviour.
- The goals or what you want to achieve with the particular child.
- What you are teaching and what the child is learning from the specific strategy selected.

Because all human beings are individuals and have different personalities, values, preferences and strengths, no one strategy or combination of strategies will be suitable for everyone. It is up to each early childhood professional to select the strategies that they feel comfortable using and work effectively for them. There are a large range of strategies available. A selection of those which are consistent with an educative, teaching and problem solving approach to behaviour management for young children are outlined below.

POSITIVE STRATEGIES FOR MANAGING THE BEHAVIOUR OF THE CHILD UNDER TWO

The cause of much behaviour which is troublesome and difficult to manage in children under two years of age can often be traced simply to being young or immaturity. Children under two rarely have learned and mastered the knowledge and skills necessary for meeting the demands of daily living. Consequently, a lot of the behaviour which early childhood professionals find they need to respond to is really to be expected developmentally and is to do with linguistic, social, emotional and intellectual immaturity. Because it is essential that young children learn to use language as part of interpersonal interaction and developing self control, early childhood professionals need to ensure that the strategy which they select for responding to infant and toddler behaviour is accompanied by a verbal comment or explanation. A number of strategies which are useful for responding to inappropriate infant and toddler behaviour are discussed below. Although these strategies may be used with older children, they are less suitable because they do not draw upon older children's emerging linguistic and intellectual competence.

Distraction

With infants and toddlers, distraction is an important strategy because it focuses on the behaviour and not the child. It recognises and respects very young children's curiosity about their environment by offering them an alternative to the inappropriate behaviour in a friendly and firm manner. For example, if an infant begins to hit a peer who is sitting close to her, the sensitive early childhood professional will offer the infant a hammer and peg board and explain what behaviour is acceptable saying, 'We hit the peg board not people.' In this way, the infant's attention is diverted to an equally appealing activity and the early childhood professional has explained and set a limit regarding what is acceptable and permissible behaviour. However, this strategy used with older children does not teach them or help them learn to select themselves alternative acceptable behaviours.

Redirection

Some determined infants and toddlers are not easily distracted and their behaviour may need to be firmly redirected by the early childhood professional. This strategy is similar to distraction because the early childhood professional makes the decision about whether a particular behaviour is unacceptable and where the young child's energy might better be directed. For example, four toddlers are working quite happily at a table using play dough. Carlos wishes to join in, but from experience the early childhood professional knows that five children at a table with that particular activity is a recipe for trouble. Consequently, she redirects Carlos' behaviour by explaining firmly and kindly that 'Only four children may work at that table. You could do a drawing now while you wait for your turn.' Alternatively, she may say 'When there is a spare chair, you may go to the dough table.' It may be necessary to take the toddler's hand and walk with him to the drawing table. Again, this strategy does not teach and help older children to use their language and problem solving skills to resolve the situation.

Offering substitutes

In order to reduce the need to say 'No' or 'Don't' to very young children, offering them a substitute activity can guide their behaviour towards more acceptable and desirable alternatives. Instead of saying to a toddler 'Don't go near the door', a responsive early childhood professional may offer the toddler a colourful picture book to look at, a hand puppet to play with or a big ball to chase after. When substitute activities are offered to very young children, the early childhood professional avoids criticising the toddler and telling him what he is doing wrong. Communicating subtly that 'I'd prefer you to play with the ball than stand by the door', in effect is teaching the toddler an acceptable alternative behaviour.

These behaviour management strategies are more meaningful for very young children than many other strategies which are more effective with children over two years of age. However, several techniques which are discussed in the following section, such as setting clear limits, rewarding appropriate behaviour, ignoring inappropriate behaviour, modelling appropriate behaviour, using natural consequences, using encouragement and identifying the goals of misbehaviour can be used effectively with infants and toddlers.

POSITIVE STRATEGIES FOR MANAGING THE BEHAVIOUR OF TWO TO FIVE YEAR OLDS

When young children are approximately two years of age, they have acquired sufficient skill in physical, language and cognitive areas of development to be responsive to a broader range of behaviour management techniques. While on some occasions early childhood professionals may still choose to use behaviour strategies which are suitable for the younger age group, such as distraction and redirection, it is important to begin to use strategies which utilise young children's emerging language and cognitive abilities. Because young children between two and five years of age have a developing capacity to use language to define, interpret, understand and reason about situations, they tend to be more rational. It is important for early childhood professionals to remember that their understanding is growing and to accept that young children will not consistently use their gradually increasing intellectual capacity to guide their behavioural choices in all situations. However, they do have some degree of self control. Consequently, early childhood professionals need to select behaviour management techniques, such as the ones outlined below, that will foster the development of self control when responding to behavioural incidents.

Setting clear limits

Because young children are learning what is acceptable and unacceptable in any situation, it is essential that early childhood professionals clearly state what they expect of children. That is, they tell children in positive terms what behaviours are acceptable and expected. Young children do not have sufficient experience to have learned what is appropriate and inappropriate and in many social situations the norms are not obvious.

The setting and articulation of clear limits for young children is part of the early childhood professional's responsibility to provide protection for them. It also meets their emotional need for safety because the boundaries create a sense of physical and emotional security for children. Although some early childhood professionals consider the setting of limits to be autocratic and restrictive for young children, giving children free rein in terms of how they behave can encourage them to engage in unacceptable behaviour in order to obtain adult intervention to bring the situation back under control. Young children need to know that adults will protect them from themselves, that is, their inability to control and regulate their own behaviour at all times and under different circumstances and also protect them from unacceptable behaviour from other children. Sensitive early childhood professionals will understand young children's need for appropriate limits. Where possible they will involve children in the establishment of the rules, boundaries and limits and explain the reasons behind them. In this way, children's need for freedom within order and choice within limits is fulfilled.

Early childhood professionals will be aware of young children's predisposition to test the limits that adults have set for them. Testing is young children's way of learning what will be accepted in a situation and how resolute adults in charge are about the limits they have set. Testing limits should not be equated with naughtiness, rather it is young children's way of determining for themselves whether the early childhood professional really means what she says. Therefore, it is important to be consistent in the setting of limits and the consequences which necessarily follow the breaking of them. The only power that the setting of limits has in influencing young children's behaviour is the certainty that consequences will follow if they are broken.

Marion (1991) outlines the characteristics of good limits. Good limits:

- Protect children's health and safety.
- Teach self control.
- Are meaningful.
- Are developmentally appropriate.
- Are stated firmly, positively and with respect.
- Have reasons behind them.

Limits can be very simple, such as 'Be careful, be kind and be safe'. Alternatively, limits may be more specific such as, 'You may look at but not touch the pot plants', 'When you go outside, you need to ask permission', 'You may turn on the cold tap in the bathroom but must not touch the hot tap', 'Toys need to be left on the grass', 'You may not hurt another child or destroy her property' and 'When we are inside, we use our quiet voices and we walk'. Too many rules and limits will be confusing for young children so the early childhood professional will only set those rules and limits which are essential for the smooth running of the day. It is important to remember that some young children will have difficulty in remembering the rules and that, on occasion, young children are so overwhelmed by what is happening at the present moment that they do not think about rules and limits in relation to their behaviour.

When young children act in accordance with the rules and limits, their behaviour can be encouraged by rewarding it.

Rewarding appropriate behaviour

Young children are not born with an innate knowledge of the rules and expectations of the culture and society in which they live. They learn them through their daily interaction with the environment and the people in it. Young children are not 'mind readers'. They do not know nor can they reliably predict what adults want or expect from them in a given situation. Most children need repeated opportunities with a given situation to really learn what is expected in that situation and to be able to produce the required behaviour when the situation presents itself in the future. The most important strategy to use in responding to young children's behaviour is to let them know when they have met adult wishes and expectations. Few adults recognise the need to teach children that they have behaved in an appropriate and acceptable manner by rewarding such behaviour. In fact, it is more common to see adults ignore and not comment on children's display of desired behaviour.

The use of reward is one of the fastest and most effective ways of teaching children what is appropriate in a given situation. Many early childhood professionals express a certain reluctance about rewarding children's behaviour because they perceive it as bribery. However, reward in this sense refers not to giving children sweets, carrots, stickers or special treats because they have behaved appropriately but rather to some sort of social acknowledgement or comment about the behaviour. Children are highly sensitive to adult attention and find it particularly satisfying and rewarding. Upon the display of appropriate behaviour, a smile, a nod, a touch, a comment such as 'I noticed that you packed the pencils up when you finished drawing. Thank you' is usually sufficient to inform a child that her behaviour was desirable, acceptable, appropriate and appreciated. Having received such positive recognition from the adult, a young child is far more likely to engage in the behaviour the next time she finishes drawing.

It is important to use reward in a careful manner. If the comment 'Good girl' is made in response to a behaviour, the message sent by the adult is a general non-specific acknowledgement of the child. It only gives half the intended message but does not take full advantage of the opportunity by relating praise to a specific behaviour. By specifying what the particular behaviour was in the acknowledgement, such as 'Thank you for wiping the paint brush before you left the easel', the child clearly understands the behaviour to which the comment related and does not erroneously ascribe it to an unrelated behaviour, such as picking her nose or dragging her jumper along the floor!

The use of a social reward is not a bribe for 'good behaviour' but a means of teaching, indicating to and informing young children about the appropriateness of their behaviour. Some early childhood professionals claim that they have spent a lot of time teaching and rewarding a certain child about a specific behaviour. It needs to be recognised that children's rates of learning vary enormously and while one child will pick up in a couple of situations what is required of her, another may take fifty to learn the same thing. Again, other children may need even a hundred opportunities with a given situation in order to understand what is expected of them and to be able to produce the appropriate behaviour in the right circumstances.

Sometimes young children do not engage in behaviour which the early childhood professional wishes to reward. In this case, it is appropriate to prompt or cue the behaviour. When it is displayed, the behaviour can be rewarded immediately. For example, it is time to clean up in preparation for lunch. The children are milling around but there has been no suggestion that it is time to wash hands before eating. The early childhood professional might comment, 'What do we do before lunch?' and at least one child will respond to this prompt saying 'Oh! We have to wash our hands first!' In this way, the early childhood professional has cued or prompted the behaviour she wishes to encourage with the use of reward.

When considering which behaviour management strategies an early childhood professional might wish to employ, the first step should always be to ask 'What does the child need to learn in the situation? How can I teach her what the expectation is in this situation?'. The next step is to become aware of any opportunity to follow the display of such behaviour immediately or as soon as possible with a social reward of some kind. In this way, early childhood professionals will be fulfilling their teaching responsibilities with young children and providing clear direction as to what behaviour was the acceptable one.

Ignoring inappropriate behaviour

As has been mentioned previously, it is very important for early childhood professionals to understand the rewarding power of adult attention on young children's behaviour. Reward needs to be used in a very specific way. Otherwise, early childhood professionals can find that they have unintentionally encouraged an undesirable and unwanted behaviour in the child. This is very easy to do. So it is essential that early childhood professionals be clear about which behaviours they wish to attend to and which behaviours they wish to ignore.

Ignoring inappropriate behaviour is a relatively easy strategy to employ in response to displays of inappropriate behaviour by young children. The early childhood professional must ensure that it is safe to ignore and withdraw attention from the particular behaviour. This strategy must never be used if a child's safety or welfare could be or is in jeopardy. For example, this strategy is never appropriate where a child is in danger of being physically hit or hurt by another child.

However, there are many commonly occurring behaviours which lend themselves to being ignored. It must be remembered that many young children are experimenting with the effects of engaging in particular behaviours, that is, they are learning about themselves and the effects of their behaviour in the environment.

Consequently, they look to the adults present to gauge their reaction. Adult reaction to any behaviour provides the young child with information about the relevance and usefulness of the behaviour. For example, children may be experimenting with a range of sounds and finally may produce a sound that resembles a swear word. Adult reaction to that sound will teach that child whether that is an important sound in the language. For most young children, they do not know the meaning of swear words, they only know that the production of the sound upsets the adults around them and gains adult attention. By ignoring the swear word, the early childhood professional is not giving any significance to the sound. Failure to gain adult attention and reaction may motivate the child to move on to try something else. Ignoring the behaviour will result in the child dropping the behaviour from her repertoire.

Unfortunately, there are three major problems with the effective use of ignoring certain behaviours as a behaviour management strategy. First, the early childhood professional may not be consistent in always ignoring the behaviour. If occasionally or even once attention is given to that behaviour, the effect will be to really strengthen the behaviour with the child unconsciously learning that she just has to engage in that behaviour more loudly, longer or more often in order to gain adult attention. This is opposite to what the early childhood professional wanted to achieve! Second, while the early childhood professional may ignore the behaviour, peers may provide the child with much attention which is also very satisfying for the child and thus may act to strengthen and encourage the persistence of the behaviour. If this is the case, then ignoring the behaviour is not the most appropriate strategy for managing the behaviour and the selection of another technique may be advised. Third, parents and other colleagues may not find ignoring the behaviour when it is safe to do so an acceptable method. In the case of swearing, many adults find it distasteful to hear young children use such words. Another strategy, such as suggesting a nonsense word or another expression to express their feelings (sugar, fiddlesticks, supercalafragilistic etc, are words frequently substituted in early childhood centres for unacceptable swear words), setting clear limits about the use of such words in the centre or teaching children a range of 'feeling language' to assist them to express and manage their feelings would be more helpful.

There are many behaviours which are suitable to be ignored, that means, pay no attention. These are behaviours which tend to be minor annoying and irritating behaviours, such as crying in order to gain attention, whining, clinging, silly antics, squabbles between children, temper tantrums, challenging and provocative comments, rude, sarcastic or angry comments, interrupting and finicky eating.

Ignoring behaviour takes some time to be effective and it may seem that the behaviour actually gets worse before it starts to diminish. But if early childhood professionals are consistent and controlled, the unwanted behaviour will be dropped eventually by the child. It is more effective if reward for appropriate behaviour is combined with ignoring inappropriate behaviour. Adults need to be cautious about forbidding or taking away a particular behaviour from a child without helping the child to find something that is acceptable in its place. For example, if children are not permitted to use swear words, they need to be given guidelines about what are acceptable ways of expressing intense feelings. This again is part of the teaching role to help young children understand what is acceptable to adults.

Modelling appropriate behaviour

Because young children are still learning cultural and societal norms and expectations, they look to the significant people in their environment to provide them with guidelines, clues and hints as to how to behave appropriately. The most powerful models for young children are their parents, other family members, the caregivers and educators in their lives, peers and the media. Children are interested and skilled observers of the behaviours of others but they are not as skilled at the interpretation of that behaviour in relation to its appropriateness.

While parental behaviour is an extremely powerful determinant of young children's, given the sheer quantity of time and the quality of most early childhood professional–child relationships, early childhood professionals also play a significant role in teaching children what is acceptable by modelling it in their own behaviour. In fact, young children pay more attention to what adults do than to what they say. Young children find it very satisfying to watch (observe) and copy (model) what early childhood professionals do. Consequently, it is extremely important that early childhood professionals are aware of and monitor their own behaviour in relation to what they want to teach young children.

If children need to learn to use quiet voices inside, then the early childhood professional needs to model this by using a quietly modulated voice in her work with children. It is inappropriate to shout across the room and then expect young children to use quiet voices only. Similarly, if the rule is that 'When we are inside, we walk, running is for outside', then it is important that the early childhood professional models this by only walking when she is inside. Again, if the rule is that chairs are for sitting on and tables are for work and eating, then the early childhood professional must ensure that she does not inadvertently sit on a table! Self control in the expression of anger can be modelled by early childhood professionals who use matter-of-fact language to express their feelings rather than being verbally explosive or physically aggressive.

It is interesting to note that, in cases where the early childhood professional's behaviour does break the rule or models unwanted behaviour, young children tend to interpret this as an invitation to themselves engage in such behaviour. Young children are more interested in adult misdemeanours than the 99.9% of cases when the adults' behaviour is consistent with expectations. Consequently, early childhood professionals need to be super-vigilant about their behaviour and ensure that they are, as far as is humanly possible, providing children with appropriate behaviours that they can copy and model.

Although young children find it inherently rewarding to model the behaviour of any adult, they tend to model more the behaviour of people with whom they have a warm, friendly and positive relationship and people who they perceive as similar to themselves and powerful (Fields and Boesser, 1994). Therefore, any early childhood professional who wishes to use modelling as a means of teaching young children how to behave in accordance with expectations, needs to establish and maintain a good relationship with young children.

Unfortunately, young children also model unacceptable behaviour which they observe in models such as same age and older peers as well as sports stars, film stars, television heroes, super heroes and computer game characters. These models sometimes display aggressive, violent and other antisocial behaviours which young children will emulate. It is important that the adults who are concerned with the development, learning and well being of young children understand their responsibility to monitor their access to negative models and to interpret and explain the unacceptable behaviours of such models in relation to normal daily life and expectations.

Modelling is a very powerful strategy for teaching young children both positive and negative behaviours. It is important that early childhood professionals remember that their positive example, that is, 'Do what I do', will encourage similar behaviour from young children rather than the telling and directing method, that is 'Do what I say'. Modelling can be used to teach concrete behaviours and skills as well as attitudes and interpersonal orientations, such as respect, empathy, fairness, feelings and self control.

Communicating with children

While Chapter 8 provides a more comprehensive discussion of the importance and role of, as well as skills for, communicating with young children, this is such an important area that it merits a summary in this section. Effective communication is the basis of effective behaviour management. However, many adults have learnt less productive means of communication and when these are employed in a behaviour management incident, they can exacerbate the situation.

It is essential that early childhood professionals learn to communicate with children respectfully (Rodd, 1989) because this is the basis of the ongoing interpersonal relationship in which the development of self control plays an important part. Many courses for the professional preparation of early childhood professionals now include specific training in those communication skills which are considered critical for such a child and family oriented profession (Rodd, 1987). It is hoped that such training will teach early childhood professionals how to avoid some of the pitfalls of behaviour management such as not listening to children, giving orders, criticising and lecturing children, failing to express their feelings genuinely and being unable to clearly express their needs, concerns, wishes, expectations and limits to children. Again, it is intended that such training will assist early childhood professionals to use communication skills which will contribute to the constructive management of a behavioural incident, such as, talking respectfully to children, using 'I' messages, specifically stating needs, wishes, expectations and limits, using active (or reflective) listening and employing win–win conflict resolution techniques.

In addition, the use of effective communication skills provides a model of good communication practice for young children. Have you noticed that many young children are not good listeners? Indeed, many adults seem to have picked up very poor listening skills during their life time. However, young children learn to become 'adult deaf' very quickly because adults tend to employ ineffective ways of talking to children. Gordon (1974: 80–87) describes these as 'roadblocks' to communication because in effect they set up barriers and obstacles to effective communication. Among others, the following communication behaviours have been identified as common examples of 'roadblocks':

- Ordering, directing, commanding.
- Warning, admonishing, threatening.
- Moralising, preaching, obliging.
- Judging, criticising, disagreeing, blaming.
- Name calling, ridiculing, shaming.
- Interrogating.
- Withdrawing, distracting, humouring.

Such communication techniques do not result in improved behaviour but rather act to diminish children's self esteem and to have a negative effect on the relationship between early childhood professionals and children. Is it any wonder then that children 'tune out'? The use of effective communication skills when managing young children's behaviour helps deal with everyday problems and incidents in a relatively harmonious atmosphere and learning environment. It also helps build and maintain open channels of communication and contact which is essential for the ongoing positive and healthy relationship between early childhood professional and child.

Warning and reprimanding young children

Warning young children is different to threatening young children with an unpleasant consequence upon the display of certain behaviours. A warning can act as prompt or a cue if it is delivered in a matter-of-fact manner. In fact, a warning can even be non-verbal.

Many early childhood professionals employ what can be called 'the look' in which they 'catch the eye' of a particular child and maintain steady eye contact for a few seconds. This technique appears to be very effective for creating an opportunity for young children to consider their present behaviour and make a choice about whether or not to continue with or change it. The message contained in 'the look' or a couple of seconds of steady eye contact includes the following non-verbal communications: first, 'I am watching you and I am aware of what you are doing'; second, 'You have a choice. You can continue with what you are doing or you can choose to do something else'; third, 'If you continue to pursue that behaviour, I will be forced to attend to it in another way'.

The use of 'the look' as a warning to young children is very helpful because it poses little threat to their self esteem, yet it sends a firm message about the inappropriateness of the behaviour and the need for the child to choose to do something different. Most young children can interpret accurately the particular behaviour to which 'the look' is directed but there is a possibility that some children will associate 'the look' with a completely irrelevant behaviour. If this is the case, then it is not a useful strategy to employ.

One limitation of the technique is that, if the child does choose to engage in a different behaviour, it may be something equally as inappropriate as the initial behaviour. Young children do not always make wise choices which meet adult expectations in terms of possible alternative behaviours. It is part of the early childhood professional's teaching role and responsibility to assist young children to choose to engage in an acceptable alternative behaviour. Otherwise, both adult and child are back in the original situation where the adult needs to warn the child that this behaviour is also unacceptable. It can become a vicious circle.

Another drawback to the effectiveness of this technique is that some children interpret 'the look' as a challenge. Their response to 'the look' is to return the warning with a provocative stare which challenges the early childhood professional to 'Come and get me! See if you can make me change my behaviour'. It is not productive to respond to a young child's challenge by getting involved in a power struggle. However, it is important that the child not believe that she has defeated the adult. One way of responding to a challenging stare back from a child might be to immediately approach the child and redirect her into another activity where more acceptable behaviour might be produced. A firm and friendly tone of voice could be used to say something like 'Alex, I see that you are ready to move to another activity now', or perhaps 'Alex, I've got an activity over here that you might enjoy', and guide the child firmly but kindly to that activity.

A warning can also be sent to a child using the tone of voice in a way that informs the child of your displeasure with a particular behaviour. The use of the child's name in a firm tone of voice will send the same message as 'the look' and is necessary in situations where children will not or do not make occasional eye contact. Whereas 'the look' is a private message between you and the child, this is a more public technique because other children will become aware of the warning message. Consequently, it is also useful for alerting the group to particular behaviours which are unacceptable in early childhood centres.

A reprimand is a verbal censure, a communication of reproof and disapproval. If a reprimand is given to a child, it needs to be done using a matter-of-fact, firm voice and focus on the behaviour rather than attack the child's character or personality. It will then have minimal effect on a young child's self esteem if the reprimand is stated using the 'I' message format. A reprimand is appropriate if a child has not responded to non-verbal or verbal warning and can be helpful to clearly point out and define the specific behaviour which meets with disapproval. For example, 'Sally, I am not prepared to let you paint at the easel if you continue to splash paint over the floor.' If a reprimand is followed with a suggestion of an acceptable alternative behaviour, such as 'You need to have less paint on your brush and stand closer to the easel', the early childhood professional has extended the reprimand into a teaching opportunity and provided the child with guidelines for overcoming the problem.

It is important for early childhood professionals to understand the limitations of common reprimands, such as 'Don't do that' or 'Stop that'. While these inform the child of your general displeasure with her behaviour, they do not inform the child about the actual behaviour to which you were referring. Neither do they offer any guidelines or suggestions about what alternative behaviours might be more acceptable. Consequently, such exclamations have marginal value in managing young children's behaviour.

Reprimands which merely criticise young children, such as 'How could you be so careless', or send angry and frustrated messages, such as 'I'm fed up with your carelessness. Stop painting now!' tend to interfere with the relationship making it hostile and distant, creating a desire in the child to lash back and can diminish a child's sense of self. They have little impact on young children's behaviour in the long term although it may appear that children do not engage in the behaviour in the short term. Giving a reprimand may not be an effective technique with children who are insecure, self critical, angry or resistant because it tends to make them angrier and more obstinate. A reprimand can be useful with young children who are reasonably secure, have a positive sense of self and good self esteem, especially if it doesn't blame, belittle or berate but rather gives a clear definition of the behaviour as well as where and how the behaviour has not met expectations.

Withdrawal of the child from the group or activity

Considerable debate and controversy surrounds the withdrawal of a child from the group or an activity for engaging in inappropriate behaviour. This strategy is often inappropriately termed 'time out' in early childhood centres. Time out is in fact a complicated tool that should only be used in a controlled situation under the guidance and supervision of a psychologist. Miller (1984:17) argues that time out is one of 'the most misunderstood and misused disciplinary methods'. The effective use of time out requires very specific implementation under strict conditions. When implemented correctly, time out can be a quick and effective means of helping children restore self control and learn to modify their behaviour. However, when implemented in an inappropriate manner, time out can be a punishing, humiliating experience of isolation and rejection where children develop feelings of resentment and hostility towards the adult who imposed the experience upon them. In some states in Australia, for example Queensland, government regulations do not allow for young children to be withdrawn from the group, out of 'the sight and sound' of the early childhood professional. Time out cannot be used in Queensland because it contravenes state regulations. In addition, the majority of early childhood professionals are not trained, neither do they have the physical conditions in their centres nor support from psychologists, to employ time out appropriately and should search for other more constructive ways for managing the behaviour of children in their care.

However, some early childhood professionals argue that withdrawal from the group or an activity is an effective option for responding to some behaviours. Withdrawal is different from time out because the child is not out of the 'sight and sound' of the early childhood professional, yet experiences a consequence of her inappropriate behaviour. Withdrawal from the group or an activity can be a valuable tool which is very effective in managing young children's behaviour. On the other hand, other early childhood professionals argue that withdrawal from the group or an activity is humiliating, punitive and does not work to change behaviour because it does not help the child learn anything about why the behaviour was inappropriate. Early childhood professionals need to be guided by professional values and standards of practice, such as the Australian and American codes of ethics, when deciding whether withdrawal is an appropriate technique for use in particular circumstances.

Early childhood professionals who support withdrawal from an activity argue that it can be a beneficial learning experience for children which fosters the development of self control when it is not threatened as a nasty punishment, the child is not isolated in a space that is frightening and its duration is for a very short time. Withdrawal from the group or an activity is a behavioural technique which is derived from learning theory and used to decrease or eliminate unwanted behaviour. It involves removing the child from the specific and immediate environment in which the unacceptable behaviour occurred. Upon a display of the unwanted behaviour, the adult clearly defines the behaviour and its consequence, for example, 'You have been knocking over other people's constructions. You need to sit by yourself quietly at another table', or 'You are fighting with the other children. You need to sit by yourself until you feel ready to play properly with them.' The child then is withdrawn immediately from the environment by the adult who is firm and friendly. As soon as the child has engaged in appropriate behaviour for a short time, say sitting quietly for five minutes, she needs to be brought back into the group with no further comment about the inappropriate behaviour. It is essential that the child be directed immediately into a group or an activity where she can be quickly rewarded for appropriate behaviour.

In this way, withdrawal from the group or an activity where the child remains in the 'sight and sound' of the early childhood professional can become a learning experience because:

- It provides young children with a definition of the unacceptable behaviour and where expectations have not been met.
- It eliminates any reward from peers in the group who might admire and encourage the flouting of rules or the challenge to adult authority.
- It gives the child time to calm down and gain self control.
- It allows the adult to settle the child into an activity where appropriate behaviour can be displayed and rewarded.

However, there are many pitfalls in terms of the effective implementation of withdrawing a child from the group or an activity in early childhood centres. First, there usually is not an appropriate place for the child to be withdrawn to. Standing in the corner or being put in the corridor is not withdrawal but unacceptably punitive for young children. The places which tend to be used for withdrawal in early childhood centres, such as the office, the bathroom, the corridor or outside may not be boring and dull. Rather, they are interesting, exciting, and entertaining because they are places where a child can explore the contents of other people's bags, eat their sweets, play with their toys, satisfy her curiosity about what is in the desk drawers, experiment with filling up the sink and flooding the bathroom, use the outdoor equipment by herself and generally get involved in equally or more unacceptable behaviour.

Some early childhood professionals have a special chair in the room to which children are sent. This does not benefit the child because she can become the centre of attention for the peer group who can direct comments towards her and inadvertently make the withdrawal experience one that the child finds very satisfying. If the peer group can be taught to ignore any one in such a chair, this may have some effect on modifying a child's behaviour because the child is not then included in the group. Most young children do not like this because being part of the group and its activities is extremely important to them.

The biggest problem with the use of withdrawal from the group or an activity is the need to be aware of the whereabouts of and the amount of time that the child has spent out of the group or activity. It is not uncommon to hear reports of children being forgotten because the early childhood professional became involved in her work with other children, leaving a child isolated at a table or in a chair by themselves for unacceptably lengthy periods. The key to withdrawal from an activity is that it is a short break from the group and its activities. For two to five year old children, withdrawal periods of between three and five minutes are recommended (Windell, 1991). Early childhood professionals who may have difficulty remembering can use a timer of some sort, such as a stop watch or egg timer. Sometimes young children can control the amount of time themselves. They can be given the responsibility to come back into the group or activity when they themselves feel that they are ready.

Certain young children are able to recognise their own need for time by themselves away from the group and will ask to be withdrawn or to go somewhere to sit by themselves. This may give an over-excited or over-stimulated child the opportunity to calm down and gain self control. One creative early childhood professional had the children paint the 'Happy Chair' where individual children could go and spend some time by themselves if they felt they needed a dose of 'happiness'! This chair was also used for those children who needed some personal space and time away from the group but the emphasis was on restoring a positive mood and acceptable behaviour.

There are some early childhood professionals who make the mistake of withdrawing a child from the group or an activity with an admonition to 'think about what you have done'. Very few young children will spontaneously go and sit in a dull and boring place and think about how their behaviour was inappropriate. Rather, they will think about how mean and nasty the adult was. While it is important for the child to understand what brought about the withdrawal from the group or activity, and to learn for the future about what behaviours are acceptable, being told to think about your behaviour while you are isolated from the group or activities is unlikely to encourage that learning.

Once a child has calmed down and become involved constructively with the group or an activity, the early childhood professional will need to find an opportunity to discuss the incident and feelings with the child. However, this should never be attempted if a child is still angry or upset or immediately after the child has been withdrawn. It is better to wait until the next day if that is the case. However, it is essential to discuss the incident at some later point, in order for the child to learn how to better handle the situation and solve the social or interpersonal problem in the future.

Withdrawal has been used for a range of behaviour, such as fighting, biting, swearing, physical and verbal aggression, angry crying and screaming, and is particularly useful for situations where an older child has lost self control and is unable to reason. Unfortunately, a child who is out of control may not leave an activity or the group willingly. If this is the case, then the early childhood professional needs to take the child firmly by the arm and physically guide her to a quiet place to sit. This does not mean using hurtful force but communicating an expectation of cooperation from the child for your wishes. The early childhood professional needs to look and sound as if she expects the child to follow her directions. If it is physically impossible to withdraw the child or if the child keeps coming back to the group or activity (say after three attempts to have the child sit quietly by herself), then this technique is not working and another strategy for managing the behaviour will need to be found.

Whether or not withdrawal is used in work with young children, it has one advantage in that the child is encouraged to learn that she will not be a member of the group if she continues to engage in certain behaviour. If used within reasonable place and time limits, and where the emphasis is upon the child re-gaining self control, it appears to have little effect on young children's self esteem. However, because some children do experience heightened emotional reactions to being excluded from the group and its activities, early childhood professionals are advised to use this strategy with caution.

Choices and consequences

Effective behaviour management with young children employs techniques that assist them to learn self control and self discipline. This involves giving children the power to make some decisions and choices about their behaviour and to experience the consequences, both natural and logical, of their behaviour. In this way, young children are encouraged to take responsibility for their behaviour. Too often, problems emerge because young children who are in the process of becoming independent are told what to do, given inflexible directions and orders and deprived of any control over their lives. When a problem occurs with a young child, especially from two years onwards, the child's cooperation is more quickly gained if a choice is offered rather than a demand being made. The essence of a quality early childhood program lies in the choices which children have in their daily lives.

The skill in offering a choice is to be very careful of the number and kind of alternatives offered. It is inappropriate for early childhood professionals to say 'What would you like to do today?' because there is not a limitless choice for young children and their often unrealistic choices will have to be denied. For example, no, we cannot go to the fun fair, neither can we paint the house, neither can we go to Mummy's work, neither can we go for a ride in the car and so on. In the same way, it is not helpful to ask 'What would you like for lunch today?' when there are only cheese sandwiches and milk available.

It is essential that young children be offered simple, realistic choices of which at least one can be fulfilled, particularly if the choices in the situation, for whatever reason, are limited. For example, the early childhood professional might offer a child who finds it difficult to settle on arrival at the centre the choice of beginning a painting or putting a puzzle together by saying, 'Good morning, Alice. Would you like to start a painting or choose a puzzle to work on now?' If Alice chooses an option which was not offered, such as to go to the dramatic play area, the early childhood professional could respond in a firm and friendly voice saying, 'That is not one of the choices at the moment'. The choices may then be repeated, for example, 'This morning we're beginning with painting or puzzles. Which one would you enjoy starting the morning with?' If Alice refuses to choose one of the two options offered in a reasonable time span, the early childhood professional will confidently make the choice for her and firmly guide her to the appropriate activity. For example, the early childhood professional might say, 'I think you might enjoy the puzzle that I have put out today'. An additional choice might be offered to Alice such as 'Will you go to the puzzle table by yourself or shall I walk there with you?' which focuses the child's attention away from the area of dispute on to another problem to be solved. If Alice continues to protest or wants to change her mind, the simplest response is to say in a firm and friendly manner, 'I'd prefer you to begin the puzzle now. When you have finished it, you may choose something else to do!'

The early childhood professional needs to think through carefully the real choices that are available in any situation. For example, what choices are really available in terms of food to eat, time to eat, activities to engage in and the time permitted in which to complete them, peer group composition and adult–child activities among others. It is unwise to offer a choice which the child is not able to take should she choose it. Adult credibility and trust is diminished by this behaviour so it is important to make it clear when there is no choice. For example, stating 'It's time to come inside now' rather than 'When do you want to come inside?' is more appropriate if there is no real choice available.

Helping children develop self control and a sense of responsibility involves giving children freedom of choice concerning their own behaviour and following their choices with appropriate consequences (Charles, 1992). The fastest learning occurs from human beings, both children and adults, experiencing the consequences of their behaviour (Balson, 1994). For example, all of us have the greatest respect for snarling dogs, hot stoves, sharp knives, slippery ice, paying the electricity bill and putting money in the parking meter because we have experienced the consequences of these events! We have been bitten, burnt, cut, fallen over, had the electricity cut off and fined!

In some ways, choice followed by consequence is giving children the opportunity to experiment with behaviour and find out for themselves what the effects of such behaviour are. There are three types of consequences.

1 **Natural consequences** are the results which follow a child's behaviour naturally and inevitably without adult intervention or interference.
2 **Logical consequences** do not occur naturally but they are related to the child's behaviour. They are designed, arranged and implemented by adults to help children learn from their choices regarding behaviour. They teach children that certain behaviours bring certain results.
3 **Artificial consequences** are imposed by adults and have no connection with behaviour. They are likely to be perceived as punishment by children. For example, if you do not eat your

lunch, you will not be allowed to play outside or if you do not pack up your blocks, you cannot ride the tricycle.

Some examples of natural consequences are:

- If a child does not eat her lunch, she will be hungry later. If she complains that she is hungry and wants something to eat, the early childhood professional can say, 'I'm sorry to hear that and I'm sure you will enjoy a snack later'. Children will only learn from natural consequences if adults do not interfere by giving the child food out of regular meal times. Under these circumstances, it is also helpful to involve the child in a positive and constructive activity so that she doesn't begin to whine and become more upset.
- If a child wears her ordinary shoes outside in the rain, then her feet will get wet and cold. Again, the early childhood professional may respond to the child's complaint about having wet and cold feet saying, 'I understand that it is unpleasant to have wet and cold feet. Tomorrow you may remember to wear your gum boots instead.'
- If a child does not wear a warm coat outside, then she will be cold.
- If a child puts her shoes on the wrong feet, it will hurt when she walks.
- If two children fight over a doll by pulling on each arm, it will break.
- If a child does not put a treasured painting away in her folio, it may disappear.

There are some natural consequences which early childhood professionals would not permit a young child to experience because they would jeopardise the safety and well being of the child. It is not permissible to let a child learn about the effects of sharp objects in power points by allowing them to stick a pencil into one. Neither should children be allowed to put their fingers near the moving blades of a fan in order to learn that it might hurt or damage your fingers and hand. Young children do not learn to swim by throwing them into a swimming pool and letting them experience the consequences of their behaviour. Neither do they learn road sense by letting them play on busy roads or cross them on their own! The responsible early childhood

154 UNDERSTANDING YOUNG CHILDREN'S BEHAVIOUR

professional would use a logical consequence or some other behaviour management strategy in such cases.

Logical consequences are used to teach social order and cooperation. They reflect the needs of the social situation and have a number of characteristics which differentiate them from punishment. Sensitive early childhood professionals design consequences which are:

- *Related* to the behaviour (the logical consequence of leaving the tricycle in the doorway is for the tricycle to be unavailable for use for a short time).
- *Respectful* (a child's favourite toys which are left out in the sand pit are unavailable because they have been put away for a period of time rather than thrown out in the rubbish).
- *Reasonable* (a child who refuses to wear a sun hat for outdoors play may only play in the shady part of the garden rather than being banned from coming outdoors).
- *Timely* (children learn fastest when adults accept the child's choice and the child experiences the consequences of their choice as soon as possible after the choice is made).

Some examples of logical consequences are:

- A child who deliberately flicks paint at children passing by will not have access to painting for the rest of the day. The early childhood professional might say, 'I'm not prepared to allow you to use the paint inappropriately. We'll try again tomorrow. You will need to choose something else to do now!'
- A child who has drawn on the wall is not permitted to use the crayons for a day. The early childhood professional may say, 'Your behaviour tells me that you've decided to move to another activity. Will you choose something yourself or will I choose for you?'
- A child who is disturbing others in a group is removed by the early childhood professional who says, 'I'm not prepared to permit you to disturb the other children's concentration. You will need to work on a puzzle by yourself now. We'll try another group activity later.'
- A child who forgets to bring her swimsuit to the centre will not be able to swim. The early childhood professional might point out, 'Only children with swimsuits will be swimming

today. I see you haven't brought your swimsuit today. You have decided to do something else this afternoon.'

- A child who does not pack up in a reasonable time has the equipment removed and will need to wait for a period of time before the equipment is available for her use. A comment might be made such as, 'Because you haven't finished packing up in a reasonable time, I've assumed that you do not want to use that equipment again today'.
- Children who do not put material away in the right place cannot find it the next day. The early childhood professional might reply in response to children's request for the material, 'It is sometimes difficult to find things when they are not put away in the right place'.

Although Gordon (1991) argues that logical consequences are the same as punishment, Adlerian writers, such as Dreikurs et al. (1964, 1982), Dinkmeyer and McKay (1980,1989), Harrison (1991) and Balson (1994) identify a range of characteristics that illustrate the ways in which logical consequences are different to punishment. The distinctions between these two techniques are discussed in Chapter 5. Logical consequences are objective, impersonal and are non-retaliatory. The implementation of consequences should be matter of fact and non-punitive. For example, for the child who has not put on her sun hat, a response could be, 'I see you've decided to play in the shade today'. The adult should have no personal involvement in the choices that the child makes but be willing to follow through consistently with the logical result of a child's choice. For example, 'You may put an apron on for cooking or choose something else to do. You decide', or 'We can have some singing, if you are settled on the mat'. An easy way to work out if you are implementing a consequence or a punishment is to listen to your tone of voice. If it is firm, friendly and matter of fact, then you are probably using a consequence. On the other hand, if it is harsh, critical, demanding and judgmental, then you are probably applying a punishment.

Identifying young children's goals of misbehaviour

One characteristic of children's behaviour which many early childhood professionals will have observed is that it is rarely random. In fact, it is usually directed towards a purpose or a goal, usually related to fitting into or finding a place in the group. Children's behaviour usually reflects attempts to be accepted by others and to develop a sense of personal significance (Charles, 1992). This point of view is a part of the Adlerian psychology which is explained by Dinkmeyer and McKay (1988), Dreikurs and Saltz (1994) and Balson (1994) in their books. Unfortunately, in their efforts to learn how to get status and recognition, young children can develop mistaken ideas about how best to belong to a group. Consequently, their goals for finding a place in the group may produce inappropriate behaviour.

Four common goals of misbehaviour which have been identified by Adler (1927) and explained by Dreikurs (1964) are:

1 *Attention seeking* or acting in a way to get undue attention from others.
2 *Power seeking* or acting in a way to get power over others.
3 *Revenge seeking* or acting in a way to hurt others.
4 *Display of inadequacy* or acting in a way to get others to leave you alone and to withdraw from the situation.

These goals tend to be sequential in order (Charles, 1992) with children who are not rewarded for, or do not get their needs met by undue attention seeking, taking up power seeking behaviours, then revenge and displays of inadequacy behaviour. Early childhood professionals need to learn how to identify the mistaken goals of misbehaviour and then act in ways which do not foster such inappropriate behaviours. Early childhood professionals need to teach children how to connect with the group, demonstrate capability and competence and find significance within a group in constructive and socially acceptable ways.

Attention seeking

Young children need and are highly sensitive to adult attention. When they believe that they are not getting sufficient attention for the behaviours that they display, they are likely to resort to trying to get attention through misbehaviour. Most adults, including early childhood professionals, are notorious for giving little or even no attention for young children's positive and desirable behaviours. Attention seeking can be active (such as being silly, overly good and conscientious, clowning around, asking a lot of questions, interrupting, whining and other behaviours which cause minor irritation in adults) or passive (such as acting shy, fearful, crying, being untidy, being lazy, clinging and other such behaviours that produce adult service for the child).

When young children demand undue attention, adults usually feel annoyed and usually respond with their first impulse which is to give the child the attention that she has demanded by her often inappropriate behaviour. Giving in to children's demand for attention at inappropriate times or for inappropriate behaviours only serves to increase the behaviour. The child erroneously believes that this has gotten her what she wants and this is her way of finding a place in the group. A better approach is to ignore a child who is inappropriately drawing attention to herself while giving attention when the child engages in appropriate behaviour. For example, ignoring a child's persistent interruptions when working with another child but commenting upon the child's effort at appropriate times, such as when she has been concentrating on building a construction without demands for attention.

Power seeking

If young children do not feel that they have found a place in the group through inappropriate attention seeking behaviour, they may resort to power seeking where they try to find importance through displays of power over others. Young children may want to show that they are the boss and in charge by defying adult authority and exerting power and control over other children. Like attention seeking, power seeking behaviour can be active (such as rebellious, defiant, disobedient behaviour including bullying, bossiness and aggressive behaviours) or passive (such as being uncooperative, going slow, being forgetful and being stubborn). Any behaviour which attempts to engage the adult or other children in a power struggle or communicates an attitude of 'try and make me' or 'try and stop me' is a display of power seeking behaviour.

When early childhood professionals come across this type of confrontational behaviour, they usually feel challenged and angry and want to show the child who is in control. Unfortunately, adults rarely come out winners in power struggles with young children and involvement in a power struggle only serves to communicate to the child that whoever is the most powerful gets what they want! A better approach is to withdraw from any conflict, confrontation, challenge or power struggle and refuse to participate in it. This does not mean that the adult has lost or given in. Rather, the adult has communicated to the child that they will not fight and that the use of power is not a way which helps a child belong in a group.

For example, a child who has been asked several times to pack up may persist with her activity. The early childhood professional may be drawn into a power struggle and finally start packing up angrily herself. Alternatively, the early childhood professional may respond with 'I don't feel like fighting with you about this today' and walk away to another group of children. If the child subsequently moves to another activity, then pack up the activity without comment in a cooperative manner yourself. However, the following day, when the child wants to play with that activity, she will be told firmly and in a matter of fact tone of voice, 'That activity is only available to children who pack it away when asked to do so. Yesterday, you chose to continue when I asked you to pack up so it is not available to you today. We'll try again tomorrow.' It is important to give young children an opportunity to demonstrate that they can engage in appropriate behaviour at a future time.

It is not easy for early childhood professionals to withdraw from power struggles with young children. However, if early childhood professionals do become involved, they are communicating to young children the value of power in life and confirming its effectiveness in getting our needs met. Young children who are defeated in power struggles by adult assertion of power are unlikely to give it up but are more likely to engage in the next goal of misbehaviour.

Revenge seeking

When young children's attempts to do whatever they like are overcome by a more powerful adult, they may wish to hurt the person who caused this situation. According to Charles (1992:68) 'hurting others makes up for being hurt'. These children erroneously only feel significant and that they belong when they hurt others and convince other people that they are unlikeable.

Young children whose behaviour is influenced by revenge in many ways set themselves up as the targets of adult anger, punishment and intervention. When the adults fulfil the child's goal by retaliating against the child's behaviour, the child's further revengeful behaviours are considered to be justified!

As with attention and power seeking behaviour, revenge seeking behaviours may be active (such as exhibitions of toughness, cruelty, violence, destructiveness and even delinquent-type behaviour) or passive (such as exhibitions of moodiness, sullenness and refusal to become involved in events). Such children may perceive themselves as disliked, pushed around, unfairly treated and insignificant and behave to generate in others considerable dislike, resentfulness, hostility and a desire to get back (Balson, 1994).

For example, a child who is revenge seeking may behave in the following way. When asked to put his book away, John retorts with a spiteful, 'It's not fair. You never let me finish what I'm doing. I hate it here and I hate you!' The early childhood professional who feels that they have been putting a lot of effort into working with John feeling special in the group might wish to retaliate with 'I'm not too keen on you either!' but will withhold this response in favour of a more constructive comment such as, 'I can see how you might feel that way but I like you'. As Marion (1991:162) reflects 'a child who seeks revenge is a child who needs help'. Instead, a wise early childhood professional will begin to work on building a better relationship with the child in order to help the child understand that she can be liked and accepted, and that she does belong to the group. Focusing on the child's acceptable behaviours rather than highlighting the child's inappropriate behaviours is one way of assisting the child to feel better about herself and to want to engage in more acceptable behaviours. However, this can be a lengthy and demoralising time while the child attempts to prove to the early childhood professional that she *really* is unlikeable and unworthy. Considerable dedication on the part of the early childhood professional is required to change the mistaken beliefs and goals of children who are seeking revenge. When children continue to feel unlovable and worthless, they may move on to the final mistaken goal which is display of inadequacy.

Display of inadequacy

Young children who have a very low sense of self worth and self esteem may attempt to convince adults that they are so unworthy that no one should bother with them. Such children believe that there is nothing that they can do well, little that they can contribute to the group, nothing to like about them and that they will fail in whatever they might try. They withdraw and remove themselves from any social or other situation which might test them. They no longer try. By displaying such behaviour, the child believes that others will not expect too much from her and leave her alone.

Many early childhood professionals may themselves feel like giving up on such a child. It is all too hard, especially if you have tried to assist this child in other ways and over a period of time. The early childhood professional may begin to believe, like the child wants them to, that it is a hopeless situation and want to give up. Yet, this is the worst response to such a child. Other common reactions are to continually point out the child's mistakes in order to 'motivate' the child, to compare them unfavourably to others and to complete or do a task for the child. All such reactions diminish the child's sense of self esteem and communicate that the child belongs to the group only if she demonstrates incompetence.

For example, a child might be asked to carry a bucket of water to the sand pit. Upon complaining that she cannot do it, the early childhood professional attempts to motivate the child by saying 'You're a big girl. All of the other children can do it so I think that you can too. Go on and take it over to the sand pit.' Whereby, the child picks up the bucket, takes a few steps and drops the bucket, splashing water over the paintings which are drying outside. The child comments 'See, I told you I couldn't do it. I don't want to be here anymore.' The early childhood professional might be tempted to make a sarcastic comment and to remind herself never to ask that child to carry water again. Alternatively, the early childhood professional might think of ways that the child can be offered opportunities to be competent and successful, thereby starting to help the child re-build her self confidence.

There are three steps to identifying the goals of misbehaviour:

1 Observe your emotional reaction to the behaviour

How do you feel? Annoyance and mild irritation suggests that the goal is attention; feeling angry, challenged and threatened indicates the power goal; feeling hurt reveals that the child's goal is revenge; and feeling hopeless and powerless indicates that the child is displaying inadequacy.

2 Observe the child's reactions to your usual way of correcting the behaviour

If the child stops the behaviour but soon resumes it, attention is the goal; if the child refuses to stop or the behaviour escalates, the child is using power; if the child becomes hostile or hurtful, revenge is the purpose of the behaviour, and if the child refuses to participate, cooperate or interact with the group, the goal is inadequacy.

3 Change your usual reaction by doing opposite to what the child expects

With attention seeking behaviour, ignore it and give attention to appropriate behaviour; for power seeking behaviour, withdraw and refuse to fight; for revenge behaviour, refuse to feel hurt and try and build a closer relationship with the child; and for displays of inadequacy, do not give up but find opportunities for the child to experience competence and success.

Children who pursue mistaken beliefs about how to belong to the group are discouraged about their ability to meet the needs of the situation in competent and socially acceptable ways. They believe that as they are now, they are not good enough. Sensitive early childhood professionals will work with such children in ways to encourage them to feel competent and capable.

Encouragement

According to Adlerian psychology, children who misbehave are discouraged children (Balson, 1994), that is, children who feel that as they are, they are not much good. They have lost their self confidence. Children become discouraged when adults focus upon their deficiencies, mistakes, errors and unmet expectations. In our efforts to help young children learn how to behave appropriately, they are told that their efforts are 'not good enough' because they are 'too messy', 'too untidy', 'too slow' and not as good as an adult would do (Balson, 1994). Such children do not believe that they can meet and cope competently and successfully with the demands of daily life. In an effort to try and overcome their sense of inferiority and to build up some sense of significance, they engage in unacceptable behaviours, show little respect for others and are uncooperative. Adult reaction to these behaviours provides further discouragement and so a vicious cycle is born.

An encouraged child is one who 'likes and respects himself and is confident about his abilities . . . a person who will respect, work well with, and help others' (Marion, 1991: 156). Such a child feels that she has a place and belongs in the group, is a useful and important contributor to group activities and is willing to cooperate to meet the needs of the situation.

There are a number of common sources of discouragement which early childhood professionals can avoid in their efforts to guide young children's behaviour towards more acceptable forms:

1   *Taking a mistake focused approach* where the child's mistakes and inadequacies are pointed out continually and corrected. For example, comments such as 'You're not holding the brush properly', 'You've got the smock on the wrong way', 'You're not holding the spoon in the right hand' and 'You've got your shoes on the wrong feet' all point to mistakes the child has made. Such fault finding is very demoralising and discouraging.

2   *Conditional acceptance* where a child is accepted, not for who she is at the present moment, but upon future improvement, such as 'When you're older, bigger, stronger, faster and can do it in the same way as an adult' teaches children to give up because they consider themselves too imperfect and inadequate to do the job in a way that will meet with adult approval.

3   *Competition with other children* where the early childhood professional highlights the differences between children by praising one and criticising the other produces children who want to belittle and disadvantage other children in an attempt to benefit and gain advantages for themselves.

4   *Certain discipline attitudes and methods* used by early childhood professionals such as overdomination or control, overprotection or pampering and underestimating the abilities of children, overindulgence or spoiling and overpermissiveness or failing to set clear limits discourage children because they prevent them from experiencing the consequences of their behaviour, learning to be independent and to find out what they can and can't do in a given situation.

There are three major ways to encourage children:

1   *To identify and focus upon strengths and assets.* All children
have strengths and characteristics which are positive even if
they are sometimes hidden and difficult to find! Early childhood professionals are advised to look for the strengths and
assets in each child and, rather than commenting upon deficiencies, to comment about the positives in a child's efforts.
For example, instead of pointing out that all the colours are
blurred in a child's painting, it is encouraging if a comment
is made about how the painting covers the whole sheet of
paper. Again, instead of commenting on a child's aggressive
outburst, it is encouraging to comment upon a child's concentrated effort at digging in the sand pit.

2   *To focus on the process not the result.* Today's children are
achievement conscious and oriented. Their parents communicate to them the importance of early achievement in most of
their activities, be they sporting or academic. When adults
focus on what children have achieved and produced, they are
teaching young children about winners (those who achieve)
and losers (those who fail to achieve). To be encouraging,
early childhood professionals need to focus upon what the
child had brought to the situation in terms of effort, improvement, enjoyment, strengths and assets. Examples of
encouraging comments are: 'You've spent a lot of time building
that tower, George', 'I can see that you are enjoying completing
the obstacle course, Katie', 'You've put a lot of effort into your
woodwork today, Vesna', 'I've noticed how helpful you've
been to the younger children during snack time, Helen' and
'You've really helped the children with their play today with
your strong singing voice, Sam' and 'Thank you for helping
me sort out the beads. You've been a big help.' Such
statements encourage children, not by focusing upon the end
product of their activity but upon what they have contributed
to the situation.

It is important that early childhood professionals understand
the differences between praise and encouragement, which are
discussed in Chapter 8. Praise is an external reward for a job
well done and teaches children that in order to be considered
worthy, then you must meet the demands, expectations and
values of others. On the other hand, encouragement is a
recognition of what children have contributed to a situation in

terms of activity, effort, enjoyment, improvement, strengths and assets (Dinkmeyer and Dreikurs, 1963).

3 *To de-emphasise mistakes and errors.* Early childhood professionals need constantly be aware that young children are still learning and as such they will make many mistakes and errors throughout the learning process. In fact, to be human is to make mistakes! Making mistakes is unavoidable but unfortunately young children are taught to be frightened of making mistakes with comments such as, 'Be careful that you do it the right way' or 'I want your best dancing in front of the parents'. Mistakes should be opportunities for learning and to improve performance. When children are afraid of making mistakes and errors, many of them do not wish to engage in the activity or make a decision in case it is wrong. Therefore, their learning opportunities are reduced and self confidence is eroded.

Encouragement is considered to be an art (Bettner, 1989) and it is quite different to praise. The distinction between praise and encouragement is summarised in Chapter 8. Early childhood professionals are practising the art of encouragement when they note young children's specific attributes, identify their specific accomplishments, point out the usefulness of their ideas, express pleasure about their activities, ask for feedback about particular issues which affect the group, help them deal with mistakes and fear of failure, show interest in the concerns they express, ask for their help, distinguish between the child and her behaviour, point out to the child what for them personally should be encouraging, express appreciation and express confidence in their ability to handle the situation.

In order to feel good about themselves, young children need much encouraging feedback in relation to whether they are doing better, improving, valued for special attributes, noticed for their efforts and getting closer to meeting adult expectations.

Inductive reasoning and problem solving

Young children are developing their capacity for understanding and reasoning, especially from two years onwards. Behaviour management is fundamentally an interpersonal problem which needs to be resolved constructively. When young children enter a group care or education setting, they are confronted with many new relationships and demands. They need to learn the skills for building and maintaining these relationships, to manage their feelings and to meet the demands of the situation. One way of helping young children to meet these expectations is to teach them inductive reasoning and problem solving skills for making relationships work and coping with various demands.

Problem solving involves teaching children to identify and define what the problem is and to think of alternative solutions and the possible effects of implementing those solutions. In this way, young children, particularly three to five year olds can be taught to use other means of resolving their interpersonal problems rather than using physical and verbal aggression. Inductive reasoning and problem solving techniques can help young children understand that certain behaviour is disliked by, hurts, or is not helpful for other people and is not useful for handling problems which come up in daily living. Young children can learn to talk about how they feel and what they want in constructive ways.

An advantage of the inductive reasoning and problem solving approach, whether used by individuals or groups of children, is, that children who have participated in finding the solution to a problem develop a sense of ownership over and are more committed to the implementation of and adherence to the solution. They also learn that there are usually a number of potential solutions to problems which occur and may learn to think about possible alternative solutions when they next encounter a problem. Miller (1984) argues that teaching young children problem solving skills contributes to the development of children's sense of responsibility, understanding of the needs of others and decision making abilities.

If early childhood professionals find children fighting over a toy, a turn on the tricycle or space at an activity, a simple solution is to turn the incident into a problem solving session. The early childhood professional may say, 'We have a problem here. There is only one tricycle and two children want to ride it at the same time. This won't work. What do you think we might do to solve this problem?' The early childhood professional is responsible for leading the children through the discussion which includes helping them generate a number of solutions, evaluate solutions, make a decision, implement the plan and evaluate the solution. Young children are likely to generate many unacceptable alternative solutions so the early childhood professional needs to be accepting but still ensure that the children understand the limitations of the unacceptable solutions. It is important to communicate to young children that a solution to the problem needs to be found and that the group will continue to search for a compromise or resolution until a choice which is acceptable to all concerned is found.

Early childhood professionals can teach problem solving to individual children either by defining the problem and suggesting a solution, such as saying 'You don't need to hit Sarah to get the doll back. Tell her what you want to happen'; 'I am not prepared to let you hurt Mary. Tell her what she did to make you angry'; and 'I can see that you're upset by what happened. How can you let her know?'. Alternatively, the early childhood professional can encourage the child to generate a solution by saying, 'Can you think of a way to work this out?', 'How could you get the children to let you be part of the game?' or 'What could you do to stop Jack from chasing you?'. It is important to check back with the child about the success of the strategy in dealing with the problem in order to help the child evaluate the outcome of this new technique as opposed to more habitual but less constructive approaches.

Teaching children problem solving skills is a way of helping them become more independent in their day to day interaction and feel more capable and responsible for managing the events in their lives. When young children have mastered the art of problem solving, they free the early childhood professional from intervening in many petty disputes and allow her more time to meet her responsibility for relating to and helping young children learn.

Some early childhood professionals complain that problem solving takes a lot of time. However, this is one of those situations where you have to spend time in order to save time! This technique is especially useful for recurring problems, ones which the early childhood professional has to deal with regularly and frequently. Instead of dealing with each individual issue, the early childhood professional is teaching a general strategy which can be applied to a range of situations and one which is an invaluable tool for older children and adults alike.

In conclusion, the techniques outlined above are ones which have been tried and found to be effective by many experienced early childhood professionals. They show respect and caring for children, do not diminish young children's sense of self esteem (and in most cases enhance it) and finally, assist children to learn, to develop self control and be responsible for the behaviour that they engage in. They are not the only techniques available but they represent a selection of the wide range of child training methods available. It is important that early childhood professionals choose and use techniques that they feel comfortable with, that are flexible for individual children and situations, that are consistent with developmental and educational goals for children, and finally, that are consistent with their philosophy of care and education.

10

WHAT WORKS FOR YOU

Creating your own approach to behaviour management

Young children develop self control or are self disciplined when they can control some of their feelings and behaviours, when they can see the potential consequences of their actions, when they can propose alternative behaviours, when they can balance their own needs with the needs of others and when they become increasingly independent in decision making with regard to appropriate behaviour to meet the needs of a given situation.

Early childhood professionals who use positive strategies to manage young children's behaviour develop a repertoire of strategies which:

- Treat young children with respect.
- Are child oriented, focusing on what the child rather than the adult needs in the situation.
- Focus on teaching and learning.
- Are empathic, nurturing and supportive.
- Incorporate long term as well as short term goals.

Such early childhood professionals understand the need for flexibility when responding to young children's behaviour that it is essential to be able to select from a range of strategies the most appropriate and effective strategy given the incident and the individual child or group of children. The strategies described in this book are derived from different, and sometimes philosophically incompatible, theoretical perspectives which include behavioural, humanistic, Adlerian and cognitive-developmental. Each of these approaches explains child development from a different perspective and recommends different ways of approaching behaviour management situations. However, as Marion (1991: 275) states, 'each approach offers valid strategies but . . . no one approach is sufficient in all cases'. It is important for early childhood professionals to remember that the overriding goal for behaviour management when selecting specific strategies is to help young children learn socially and culturally appropriate behaviour. Therefore, from time to time, they may choose strategies from seemingly incompatible approaches to respond to specific children and incidents. As long as they are aware of the young children's developmental needs and limitations, the theoretical basis of the strategy, appropriate ways to use the strategy and any potential outcomes of the strategy for young children, then early childhood professionals are likely to use behaviour management strategies which are developmentally appropriate.

According to Marion (1991), early childhood professionals will choose as part of their repertoire behaviour management strategies which will help children:

- Feel safe and secure.
- Build self esteem.
- Be self responsible.
- Foster self control.
- Develop competence.
- Encourage empathy.
- Stimulate thinking and reasoning on the part of young children.

Furthermore they:

- Are clear about their values and expectations concerning children's behaviour, particularly what they will and will not accept.
- Feel confident about and willing to set clear rules, limits and guidelines.
- Respond to behavioural incidents predictably and consistently.

In this way, early childhood professionals who use positive behaviour management strategies expect, and are sometimes rewarded with, developmentally appropriate and often mature behaviour from young children.

When early childhood professionals create their own repertoire of behaviour management strategies, they are using what is described as an eclectic approach. However, some early childhood professionals do not really understand the theoretical basis of the techniques that they employ, do not utilise them in the appropriate manner, with the right child or in a suitable situation (Rodd and Holland, 1990). Consequently, the results which they expect do not occur. They may not understand fully that certain management techniques are more suitable for producing or teaching certain behaviours in young children. Managing young children's behaviour effectively is an intellectual and emotional challenge for early childhood professionals who have a responsibility to select a management strategy which is likely to be most effective for a specific child at a specific time. This requires that the early childhood professional understand the needs of all the individual children in the group, be aware of and understand the effects of a range of different management techniques, be skilled in the application of specific techniques and be flexible in her approach to responding to individual children, circumstances and behavioural incidents.

In order to create your own approach to managing young children's behaviour, the following steps are useful:

1   Learn about child and family development, current educational approaches to teaching and learning in the early years and ways to establish and maintain interpersonal relationships.
2   Develop your personal philosophy of early care and education of young children on the basis of your personal and professional values and the theoretical perspectives that you feel reflect these values.
3   Understand the short term, long term and educational goals that you have for individual children and a group of children.
4   Get to know and understand the needs, abilities, interests, strengths and developmental levels of the individual children in the group.
5   Establish a small number of clear rules with related consequences to ensure the smooth running of the centre.
6   Select and become competent in the use of a range of positive management techniques that match your values, philosophy and goals for young children, enhance their self esteem and teach them to be competent, cooperative and responsible members of the group.

7 Develop sufficient skill in the application of a range of positive management techniques to permit a flexible approach for dealing with the problem at hand and the particular child.

8 Monitor your responses to behavioural incidents and reduce the use of ineffective management techniques as well as those which have detrimental effects upon young children's self esteem.

9 Remember that you are human too and will make mistakes in responding to behavioural incidents. Treat any mistakes as a learning opportunity and ask yourself 'How could I have responded differently?', 'What other options were there in the situation?' or 'What would have worked better or been more effective?' There will be many other opportunities in your work with young children for you to practise your behaviour management repertoire.

A number of other guidelines are helpful to keep in mind when responding to young children and their behaviour:

1 Use clear and simple language to communicate wishes and expectations to children.

2 Make only one reasonable request or command at a time.

3 Avoid making too many requests or giving too many commands in any one session. Search for alternative ways of encouraging the desired behaviour.

4 Make a request, state a rule or give a warning only once then take action. It is the certainty of adult action, whatever it is, that governs young children's behaviour.

5 Make sure that you follow the rules too.

6 Allow young children a reasonable amount of time to meet your request or comply with your directive. Do not expect young children to 'jump to' but ensure that they do not employ delaying tactics.

7 Select management techniques that will encourage cooperative attitudes and behaviour in young children.

Windell (1991) has developed a number of helpful categories under which the purposes of selected behaviour management techniques may be classified. Most of these have been discussed in the preceding chapters of this book. An adaptation of Windell's categories is presented below.

Techniques that prevent early problems

Take a learning approach to behaviour management and teach limits.
Use a problem prevention approach and childproof the centre.
Focus on the behaviour not the child.
Repeat rules often.
Avoid sudden changes and cue children for changes in activities and routine.
Anticipate and ward off problems from occurring.
Offer limited choices.
Give children some latitude to make mistakes.

Techniques that prevent later problems

Examine the environment in terms of problem prevention.
Offer limited choices.
Prompt children to remember rules by giving them cues or reminders.
Establish and teach routines.
Plan in advance.
Define and communicate clear limits.
Make new rules as the situation requires.
Use problem solving.

Techniques that foster self control

Ignore behaviour if safe and appropriate to do so.
Cue or prompt acceptable behaviour.
Use humour.
Provide encouragement.
Use natural and logical consequences.
Use reasoning.
Use problem solving.

Techniques that encourage desired behaviour

Communicate rules and limits in a clear and friendly manner.
Give attention to positive behaviours that are to be encouraged.
Reward positive behaviours.
Prompt desired behaviours so that they may be rewarded.
Model appropriate behaviours.
Provide encouraging feedback and comments.
Use problem solving.

Techniques that discourage unacceptable behaviour

Ignore inappropriate behaviour when it is safe to do so.
Give 'the look'.
Use withdrawal from the group or an activity.
Withhold rewards and privileges.
Give a warning or reprimand.
Use natural and logical consequences.
Identify the goals of misbehaviour and respond accordingly.

Early childhood professionals need to become familiar with the purposes of each of their selected strategies and what they are likely to achieve when applied to behavioural incidents.

Some final recommendations which have been adapted from Feldman (1991) may be helpful as short reminders of what not to do as well as what to do when early childhood professionals are involved in a behaviour management incident. These are:

Avoid

Yelling and screaming.
Use of physical punishment.
Power struggles.
Expecting perfection.
Embarrassing or humiliating a child in public.
Threatening or making empty promises.
Comparing children.
Arguing.
Putting off dealing with a problem.

Try to

Give clear, simple and minimal rules and limits.
Discipline in private and with a cool head.
Be fair, firm and kind.
Be consistent.
Give lots of rewards, praise and encouragement.
Prevent problems from occurring.
Act promptly—'more action, less talk'.
Give choices and allow children to experience their consequences.
Use another strategy if what you are doing is not working.
Understand young children's developmental capabilities.
Respect children.
Listen to children and encourage them to verbalise their feelings.
Follow through.
Be warm, caring and friendly.

In conclusion, it will take many years for young children to learn the norms and skills to become self controlled and self disciplined in their community and society. Progress may be slow! However, it is recognised that there are ways of working with young children which are more beneficial for helping them learn appropriate behaviour and for the development of their self esteem. A well thought-out combination of curricula, time, space, and approaches to learning offered in a harmonious emotional atmosphere will help create an environment that is conducive to young children's development and learning. The approaches outlined in this book are by no means the only ones available but represent a selection of easily learned, easily implemented and successful approaches to behaviour management. Given the complexity of this subject, early childhood professionals are encouraged to read the range of material that is available to broaden their understanding about different approaches.

Early childhood professionals put a lot of time and effort into dealing with children's behaviour in care and educational settings. They are not always in circumstances which permit them choice when responding to behavioural incidents. Old established habits can be difficult to change! Nevertheless, in order to overcome the sense of helplessness and feelings of demoralisation which can pervade efforts at behaviour management, early childhood professionals need to be aware that there are options available and that, with practice and determination, they can develop a confident and workable system of behaviour management.

References

Adler, A. 1927 *The Practice and Theory of Individual Psychology*, Harcourt, Brace and Co, New York

Albert, L. 1989 *A Teacher's Guide to Cooperative Discipline. How To Manage Your Classroom and Promote Self Esteem*, American Guidance Service, Circle Pines

Alper, J. 1989 'The roots of morality', *Human Development 87/88. Annual Editions*, ed, H.E. Fitzgerald, Dushkin, Connecticut

Artmann, S. 1979 'Morals or mouthings: caregiver interaction makes all the difference', *Childhood Education*, 56, 31–5

Australian Early Childhood Association Inc. 1991 'Australian Early Childhood Association Code of Ethics', *Australian Journal of Early Childhood*, 16, 1, 3–6

Balson, M. 1994 *Becoming Better Parents*, 4th edn, Australian Council for Educational Research, Melbourne

Bandura, A. 1977 *Social Learning Theory*, Prentice Hall, Englewood Cliffs

Berk, L. 1991 *Child Development*, 2nd edn, Allyn and Bacon, Needham Heights

Bettner, B. L. 1989 *An Adlerian Resource Book*, North American Society of Adlerian Psychology, Chicago

Biddulph, S. 1994 *The Secret of Happy Children*, rev edn, Bay Books, Sydney

Bredekamp, S. ed. 1987 *Developmentally Appropriate Practice in Early Childhood Programs Serving Children from Birth through Age 8,*

National Association for the Education of Young Children, Washington

Bremner, J.G. 1994 *Infancy*, 2nd edn, Blackwell Publishers, Oxford

Buzzelli, C.A. 1992 'Young children's moral understanding: learning about right and wrong', *Young Children*, 47, 6, 47–53

Campos, J.J., Barrett, K.C., Lamb, M.E., Goldsmith, H.H. and Stenberg, C. 1983 '"Socioemotional development", infancy and developmental psychobiology', eds M.M. Haith and J.J. Campos, *Handbook of Child Psychology*, 4th edn, vol 2, ed. P.H. Mussen, Wiley, New York

Charles, C.M. 1992 *Building Classroom Discipline*, 4th edn, Longman, New York

Clewett, A.S. 1988 'Guidance and discipline: teaching young children appropriate behaviour', *Young Children*, May, 26–31

Clyde, M. and Rodd, J. 1989 'Professional ethics: there's more to it than meets the eye!' *Early Child Development and Care*, 53, 1–12

Damon, W. 1977 *The Social World of the Child*, Jossey-Bass, San Francisco

Davenport, G.C. 1994 *An Introduction to Child Development*, 2nd edn, Collins Educational Publishers, London

Dinkmeyer, D. and Dreikurs, R. 1963 *Encouraging Children to Learn: The Encouragement Process*, Prentice Hall, Englewood Cliffs

Dinkmeyer, D. and McKay, G.D. 1989 *Systematic Training for Effective Parenting*, American Guidance Service, Circle Pines

Dinkmeyer, D. and McKay, G.D. 1980 *Systematic Training for Effective Teaching*, American Guidance Service, Circle Pines

Dreikurs, R., Grunwald, B. and Pepper, F. 1982 *Maintaining Sanity in the Classroom*, Harper and Row, New York

Dreikurs, R. and Soltz, V. 1964 *Children: The Challenge*, Hawthorne Books, New York

Eisenberg, N.C. 1992 *The Caring Child*, Harvard University Press, Cambridge

Erikson, E. 1963 *Childhood and Society*, 2nd edn, Norton, New York

Feldman, J.R. 1991 *A Survival Guide for the Pre school Teacher*, Centre for Applied Research in Education, New York

Fields, M.V. and Boesser, C. 1994 *Constructive Guidance and Discipline. Preschool and Primary Education*, Macmillan, New York

Gartrell, D. 1995 'Misbehaviour or mistaken behaviour?' *Young Children*, 50, 5, 27–34

Glasser, W. 1992 *The Quality School*, 2nd edn, Harper and Row, New York

Gordon, T. 1970 *Parent Effectiveness Training*, P.H. Wyden, New York

Gordon, T. 1974 *Teacher Effectiveness Training*, P.H. Wyden, New York

Gordon, T. 1991 *Teaching Children Self-Discipline at Home and at School*, Random House, Sydney

Grossman, H. 1995 *Classroom Behaviour Management in a Diverse Society*, 2nd edn, Mayfield, California

Harrison, J. 1991 *Understanding Children: Towards More Responsive Relationships*, Australian Council for Educational Research, Melbourne

Herbert, M. 1987 *Behavioural Treatment of Children with Problems: A Practice Manual*, 2nd edn, Academic Press, London

Hoffman, M.L. 1970 *Carmichael's Manual of Child Psychology*, ed. P.H. Mussen vol 2, 3rd edn, John Wiley and Sons, New York

Honig, A.S. 1985 'Compliance, control and discipline. Review of research', *Young Children*, January, 50–8

Houghton, D. and McColgan, M. 1995 *Working With Children*, Collins Educational Publishers, London

Kamii, C. 1984 'Obedience is not enough', *Young Children*, May, 11–14

Kuhmerker, L. 1976 'Social interaction and the development of right and wrong in young children', *Journal of Moral Education*, 5, 3, 257–64

Lerman, S. 1984 *Responsive Parenting*, American Guidance Service, Circle Pines

Maccoby, E.E. 1988 *Social Development. Psychological Growth and the Parent–Child Relationship*, Harcourt Brace Jovanovich, New York

Marion, M. 1991 *Guidance of Young Children*, 4th edn, Macmillan, New York

Marshall, H.H. 1989 'The development of self concept', *Young Children*, July, 44–51

Meade, A. 1995 'Good Practice to Best Practice. Extending Policies and Children's Minds', keynote address presented at the Start Right 95 Conference, September, Royal Society for the Encouragement of the Arts, Manufacture and Commerce, London

Miller, C.S. 1984 'Building self-control. Discipline for young children', *Young Children*, November, 15–19

National Association for the Education of Young Children 1984 *Accreditation Criteria and Procedures of the National Academy of Early Childhood Programs*, National Association for the Education of Young Children, Washington

National Childcare Accreditation Council of Australia 1993 *Putting Children First. Handbook for the Quality Improvement and Accreditation System,* Commonwealth of Australia, Canberra

Office of Preschool and Child Care 1992 *Early Childhood Curriculum Guidelines,* Government Printing Office, Melbourne

Pardeck, J.T. 1988 'A seminar for teaching new discipline techniques to parents', *Early Child Development and Care,* 34, 41–61

Piaget, J. 1971 *The Construction of Reality in the Child,* Ballantyne, New York

Pulkkinen, L. 1982 'Self-control and continuity from childhood to late adolescence', *Life Span Development and Behaviour,* eds P. Bates and O. Brim, vol 4, Academic Press, New York

Rodd, J. 1987 'It's not just talking. The role of interpersonal skills training in the preparation of early childhood educators', *Early Childhood Development and Care,* 29, 2, 241–2

Rodd, J. 1988 'Helping each other: the effects of cost, need and contextual factors upon preschoolers' helping behaviour', *Early Child Development and Care,* 39, 53–66

Rodd, J. 1989 'Better communication = better relationships', *Day Care and Early Education,* 17, 1, Fall, 28–9

Rodd, J. and Holland, A. 1990 'Am I doing the right thing? What else could I do? Approaches to child management', *Australian Journal of Early Childhood,* 15, 4, 28–34

Rodd, J. and Millikan, J. 1994 'Parental perceptions of early childhood services for pre-primary children in Australia', *Early Child Development and Care,* 101, 89–100

Rogers, W.A. 1989 *Making a Discipline Plan: Developing Classroom Management Skills,* Nelson, Melbourne

Sabatino, D. 1991 *A Fine Line: When Discipline Becomes Child Abuse,* TAB Books/McGraw Hill, Summit

Schaffer, H.R. 1990 *Making Decisions About Children. Psychological Questions and Answers,* Blackwell Publishers, Oxford

Schiller, W. and Cohen, D. 1988 'Curriculum in early childhood centres', *Curriculum Perspectives,* 8, 1, 31–8

Soderman, A.K. 1985 'Dealing with difficult young children. Strategies for teachers and parents', *Young Children,* July, 15–20

Smith, A. 1993 'Early childhood educare: seeking a theoretical framework in Vygotsky's work', *International Journal of Early Years Education,* 1, 1, 47–61

Stengel, S.R. 1982 'Moral education for young children', *Human Development 89/90 Annual Editions*, ed. H.E. Fitzgerald, Dushkin, Connecticut

Straughan, R. 1991 *Can We Teach Young Children to be Good? Basic Issues in Moral, Personal and Social Education*, Open University Press, Bristol.

Thomas, A. and Chess, S. 1977 *Temperament and Development*, Brunner/Mazel, New York

Turner, P.H. and Hamner, T.J. 1994 *Child Development and Early Education. Infancy Through Preschool*, Allyn and Bacon, Needham Heights

Vygotsky, L.S. 1962 *Thought to Language*, MIT Press, Cambridge

Vygotsky, L.S. 1978 *Mind in Society: The Development of Higher Mental Processes*, Harvard University Press, Cambridge

Webb, P.K. 1989 *The Emerging Child. Development Through Age Twelve*, Macmillan, New York

Windell, J. 1991 *Discipline. A Sourcebook of 50 Failsafe Techniques for Parents*, Macmillan, New York

INDEX

77; eclectic, 170; humanistic, 77
Thomas, A. & Chess, S., 29
time out, 142
Turner, P.H. & Hamner, T.J., 18, 31

values, xv; code of ethics, 72; professional, 12, 70, 72; standards of practice, 72
Vygotsky, I.S., 34

Webb, P.K., 2, 102, 112, 131
Windell, J., 7, 149, 171

Also by Jillian Rodd

LEADERSHIP IN EARLY CHILDHOOD

The Pathway to Professionalism

With community insistence on quality early childhood care and education in a time of diminishing resources, professionalism has become a major issue in early childhood. To date, few authors have tackled the task of defining what leadership means in early childhood using terminology that practitioners can understand.

Leadership in Early Childhood is a practical resource for early childhood professionals who want to understand the role of leadership in early childhood. Drawing on her extensive experience in the field, Jillian Rodd presents a framework for understanding the demands of leadership and for developing skills that are relevant to the early childhood context.

PUBLISHED IN AUSTRALIA BY ALLEN & UNWIN

PUBLISHED IN NORTH AMERICA BY TEACHERS COLLEGE PRESS

PUBLISHED IN THE UK BY OPEN UNIVERSITY PRESS